THE NATIONAL GALLERY OF SCOTLAND

CONCISE CATALOGUE OF PAINTINGS

Gallery interior showing Room IV, 1997, photographed by Douglas MacGregor

The National Gallery of Scotland
Concise Catalogue
of Paintings

THE TRUSTEES OF THE NATIONAL GALLERIES OF SCOTLAND

EDINBURGH 1997

Designed by Gerald Cinamon, London
Typeset by Kitzinger, London
Printed by BAS Printers Ltd, Over Wallop, Hampshire
ISBN 0 903598 65 5

Cover illustrations

Front: *An Allegory (Fábula)* (detail) by El Greco
Back: *Diego Martelli* (detail) by Edgar Degas

Photographic credits
Antonia Reeve
Jack Mackenzie
Tom Scott

CONTENTS

INTRODUCTION AND ACKNOWLEDGEMENTS

This is the first fully illustrated concise catalogue of the National Gallery of Scotland's collection of paintings. The earliest complete catalogue of the Gallery's collection was written by W. B. Johnstone RSA, the first curator, and published in 1859. Fifty-one editions were issued, the last revised version being published in 1957. This was followed by the *Shorter Catalogue* published in 1970, its supplement of 1976 and revision of 1978, and *Illustrations*, published in 1980. This present catalogue replaces previous ones as the most accurate and current listing of the collections and marks the transfer of the Gallery's records onto computer. It continues the series of permanent collection concise catalogues published by the National Galleries of Scotland, which already comprises *The Concise Catalogue of the Scottish National Portrait Gallery* (1990) and *The Concise Catalogue of the Scottish National Gallery of Modern Art* (1993). The revised edition of *Italian and Spanish Paintings in the National Gallery of Scotland* was published in 1993 and catalogues of the National Gallery's collections of Scottish Drawings and its French Paintings are currently in preparation. The aim of the series of concise and school catalogues is to make the collections of the National Galleries of Scotland known to as wide a public as possible.

We are most grateful to all those who helped in the compilation and checking of the catalogue: Aidan Weston-Lewis, Helen Smailes and above all to Julia Lloyd Williams who has acted as editor and supervised the whole project. We should also like to thank Deirdre Perth who assembled the necessary photographs with great patience and Julia Rayer Rolfe who organised the new photography undertaken by Antonia Reeve and Jack Mackenzie. The technicians and conservators of the National Galleries of Scotland have also helped with unframing works, measuring and providing necessary data. The task of transferring the Gallery's records onto computer and entering updated information was carried out by Valerie Hunter. Her attention to detail has been invaluable. We are also most grateful to Janis Adams for supervising this publication and to Gerald Cinamon and Tony Kitzinger for its design and typesetting. Any catalogue of this type also relies on the work of previous curators of the collection and we thank them as well as the many experts who have kindly helped in providing the compilers with information and advice.

TIMOTHY CLIFFORD
Director
of the National Galleries of Scotland

MICHAEL CLARKE
Keeper
of the National Gallery of Scotland

View of the National Gallery (on left) and the Royal Scottish Academy (on right), c. 1900,
photographed by Thomas Annan

THE ORIGINS AND FOUNDATION
OF THE
NATIONAL GALLERY OF SCOTLAND

The National Gallery of Scotland, the principal of the three National Galleries of Scotland, houses the national collections of European and Scottish art *c.* 1300–1900. The building, situated on the Mound causeway which links Edinburgh's Old and New Towns, was designed by William Henry Playfair (1790–1857). Opposite, to the north, stands its predecessor, the former Royal Institution building (now the Royal Scottish Academy) also designed by Playfair.

The Royal Institution was founded in Edinburgh on 1 February 1819 as the Institution for the Encouragement of the Fine Arts in Scotland and received its Royal charter in 1827. Apart from the short-lived Academy of Saint Luke (1729–31), the other main body concerned with the fine arts in Edinburgh was the 'Honourable Board of Trustees for Fisheries, Manufacturers and Improvements in Scotland'. More commonly known as the 'Board of Manufactures', this was a government department whose origins lay in the Treaty of Union of 1707. In the hope of promoting better design, the Board of Manufactures had set up the drawing school known as the Trustees' Academy in Edinburgh in 1760, first occupying rooms lent by Edinburgh University and later moving to Picardy Place in 1806. Originally teaching drawing to artisans, this subsequently expanded its curriculum, later training artists such as David Wilkie.

The rather more autocratic Institution also aimed to promote artistic enlightenment, but through loan exhibitions rather than teaching. Its first exhibitions were held in 1819 and 1820 at the painter 'Mr Raeburn's Gallery' at York Place and showed works by artists such as Van Dyck, Rembrandt, Poussin and Velázquez. The paintings were predominantly drawn from private collections of the numerous aristocratic members of the Institution, such as the Earls of Elgin, Wemyss and Hopetoun. The display was organised by the Manager of the Trustees' Academy, the artist Andrew Wilson. Later exhibitions in 1821, 1822, 1824 and 1825 also showed contemporary artists' work at Bruce's Gallery in Waterloo Place.

The popularity of these exhibitions and the growing collection of casts acquired by the Trustees' Academy were amongst the pressing reasons for the need for a larger venue and resulted in the commission of the Institution building. It was paid for by the Board of Manufactures, who were funded by the Treasury, and completed in 1826. The Board of Manufactures' Trustees' Academy, together with the Institution, the Scottish Society of Antiquaries and the Royal Society of Edinburgh made up the the building's first occupants. The series of purpose-built exhibition rooms provided a permanent suite of display galleries for the Institution which held a successful inaugural exhibition of modern works there in February 1826, followed by an Old Masters exhibition two months later. However, complaints about the exclusivity of the Institution and its attitudes, together with claims that income from contemporary exhibitions was being vired to Institution funds (rather than benefitting the artists concerned), led to a dissatisfied group of artists and their supporters setting up a self-governing body, the Scottish Academy, in 1826. They held alternative exhibitons of their own in Waterloo Place. This group received its Royal charter in August 1838 and subsequently became known as the Royal Scottish Academy (RSA).

The withdrawal of the support of many contemporary Scottish artists who allied themselves to the Scottish Academy meant that the Institution was presented with fewer modern works for its own exhibitions. Accordingly the Institution ceased 'modern' painting exhibitions in 1830 and began to devote its energies to building up a permanent collection of Old Masters. Though the Royal Institution committee had been buying pictures from living Scottish artists by 1827, during 1830–31 they bought thirty-eight 'Ancient Pictures' in Italy using an accumulation of funds released specifically for the purpose. The negotiations were concluded by Andrew Wilson who had been sent to Italy by the Royal Institution to seek out and purchase outstanding paintings, including Van Dyck's *'The Lomellini Family'* and his *St Sebastian Bound for Martyrdom*, which formed the nucleus of the collection of Old Master paintings. This was later augmented by the collection of Sir James Erskine of Torrie (1772–1825). The Torrie Collection (which was made up of some important Italian and Dutch works, such as Jacob van Ruisdael's *The Banks of a River*, as well as a number of fine sculptures and casts) was entrusted to Edinburgh University in 1835, but responsibility for display was subsequently passed on to the Board of Manufactures in the Torrie Agreement of 1845. (The Torrie Collection is now at the Talbot Rice Gallery in the University of Edinburgh, although the Ruisdael and some sculptures still remain on display at the National Gallery of Scotland. Other pictures which belonged to Sir James Erskine are now on long term loan to Duff House, Banffshire, an outstation of the National Galleries of Scotland.)

The Scottish Academy also began to form a collection of pictures, mainly of the British school, with its purchase of some large paintings by William Etty in 1829–30. With the notable exception of Bassano's *The Adoration of the Kings*, they bought virtually no other Old Masters. By 1835 the Scottish Academy's contemporary exhibitions were also proving extremely popular and they lacked sufficient space in their rented Waterloo Place rooms. Their members were looking for a larger exhibition venue and in 1835 finally gained permission from the Board of Trustees to lease some of the galleries in the Royal Institution building for a certain part of the year, as well as gaining access to other facilities such as the library and cast collection. But space was at a premium and wrangles ensued about what the Academy was entitled to in its lease. Finally appeal was made to the Treasury in London and, in a report of 13 December 1847, Mr John Shaw Lefevre, Secretary of the Board of Trade, tried to find a solution in his recommendation that the Royal Scottish Academy should be provided with galleries for their exhibitions. A second report of 1849 ordered the Board of Manufactures to find part of the funding necessary to build these galleries and it was also stated that the Royal Institution collection should be handed over to form the core of a new Scottish National Gallery, along with the Torrie Collection.

The foundation stone of the National Gallery of Scotland was laid on 30 August 1850 by H.R.H. Prince Albert and the building opened to the public on 22 March 1859. The site was granted by the City of Edinburgh and construction cost £50,000, of which £20,000 was raised by the Board of Manufactures and £30,000 by the Treasury. For about five years before the opening, the Royal Institution building was used to stockpile

*Interior of the National Gallery
in 1883 by Arthur E. Moffat*

works being collected for the new gallery through bequests and gifts and some of these were put on display there. The new National Gallery building was originally shared with the Royal Scottish Academy, which occupied the eastern side of the two main suites of octagonal rooms. (The same arrangement also originally existed in London with the National Gallery in Trafalgar Square sharing half of the building with the Royal Academy from 1837, until the latter moved to Burlington House in 1868.) The Royal Scottish Academy side was completed and occupied by 1855 but, although finished by 1856, the western side remained empty for a few more years. The pictures ultimately intended for display there remained at the Royal Institution and it was not until September 1858 that they were finally brought over to their new building and installed. The decorative design for the new gallery had been devised by David Ramsay Hay in consultation with the architect and comprised claret-painted walls with green 'Dutch weave' flooring (the colour scheme re-instated in the Gallery in the 1980s).

The Royal Scottish Academy had been permitted to use the eastern suite of rooms for its loan exhibitions for four months and for showing its Diploma collection for the rest of the year. On the western side, the National Gallery's collection continued to grow and although a number of works were transferred in 1889 to the new National Portrait Gallery designed by Rowand Anderson in Queen Street, space was still severely limited. In 1903 a departmental committee reported upon the administration of the Gallery building and it was finally suggested that the National Gallery should take over the whole of the premises on the Mound and that the Royal Institution should be refurbished and given over for the use of the Royal Scottish Academy.

   The National Gallery of Scotland Act was passed in Parliament in 1906. In the place of the Board of Manufactures this created a Board of Trustees of the National Gallery of Scotland, together with a Chairman, Director and Keeper, though appointments to these posts were only completed in April 1907. On 12 January 1910, a Parliamentary Order ('The Appropriation of Buildings', following the 1906 Act), finally gave tenancy to the Academy of the Royal Institution building free of rent in exchange for their half of the Gallery building. In order to clear the Institution building for the Royal Scottish Academy, it was necessary to find alternative accommodation for the four institutions which were then housed there, including the old gallery of casts and the former Trustees' Academy school of art (known after 1858 as the School of Art of the Board of Manufactures). The ownership of all the Royal Scottish Academy's collection of works of art (with the exception of Diploma works) was also transferred to the new Board of Trustees of the National Gallery of Scotland. This included part of the substantial collection once owned by the antiquarian David Laing whose 2,282 drawings were to form the nucleus of the Gallery's holdings in graphic art (now amounting to some 18,000 prints and drawings).
   Alterations were then made to the National Gallery building to unite the two suites of rooms into a single gallery and to create one entrance and hall (where previously there had been two) in the north portico. The designs were made by William Thomas Oldrieve (1853–1922) and the completed scheme, including a new upper gallery, which had formerly housed the Royal Scottish Academy's Life School classes, and a staircase up to it, was opened to the public on 3 June 1912. The integrated display of works of art in the National Gallery of Scotland consisted of those pictures purchased by or given to the

The upper gallery and oculus (left, now Room A1) and front staircase (right) designed by William Thomas Oldrieve, photographed c. 1912

Royal Institution, sculptures and pictures from the Torrie Collection, works acquired by the Board of Manufactures, modern works bought by the Royal Association for the Promotion of the Fine Arts (which were put on loan and subsequently presented to the Gallery in 1897), the transferred Royal Scottish Academy works and, not least, paintings given or bequeathed to the National Gallery itself, some gifts dating from before 1859.

From its earliest days the Gallery has benefitted from outstanding donations of works of art. As the inaugural catalogue of 1859 stated: 'the maintenance and extension of this National Collection must always, in a great measure, depend on the public spirit and liberality of individuals, there being no fixed revenue or public funds devoted to the purchase of pictures'. This 'public spirit and liberality' resulted in Lady Murray of Henderland's bequest of fifteen paintings in 1861, Mrs Nisbet Hamilton Ogilvy of Biel's bequest of twenty-eight pictures in 1921, and the 11th Marquess of Lothian's bequest of eighteen works in 1941. Other gifts included masterpieces such as Frans Hals's *Verdonck*, Rembrandt's *A Woman in Bed* and the twenty-one superb works by Monet, Gauguin, Degas and other Impressionist and Post-Impressionist artists from the 1960 gift and 1965 bequest of Sir Alexander Maitland in memory of his wife Rosalind. It was only in 1903 that the Gallery received its own purchase grant, initially of £1000. Further opportunities for acquisitions were given by the Cowan Smith Bequest of 1919, which provided a fund of £55,000, producing an income which quadrupled the Gallery's annual grant. Amongst the most notable purchases made in subsequent years were those of Gauguin's *The Vision after the Sermon* (1925) and Degas's *Diego Martelli* (1932). Substantial bequests of money were also given by Sir David Young Cameron and John Stewart Michie in 1945 and 1954.

The National Gallery of Scotland from Princes Street Gardens

The complexity of funding acquisitions has greatly increased in the last fifty years and the prices of outstanding works of art have outstripped inflation. Velázquez's *An Old Woman Cooking Eggs* was acquired for £57,000 from the Cook collection in 1955 with the aid of the National Gallery's grant in aid, the National Art Collections Fund and various trust funds. At that time it was the Gallery's most expensive purchase. That distinction is currently held by a work of sculpture, Canova's *The Three Graces,* jointly acquired with the Victoria and Albert Museum with the aid of many funding bodies based on a gross valuation in excess of seven million pounds. The most expensive painting acquisition to date has been the Guercino *Tancred and Erminia,* acquired last year by Private Treaty sale from the estate of the late Lord Howard of Henderskelfe with the aid of the Heritage Lottery Fund, the National Art Collections Fund, a special Scottish Office grant and many public and private donations raised by a very vigorous campaign. With the severe reduction of its purchase grant in recent years the Gallery is heavily dependent upon the support of bodies such as the Heritage Lottery Fund and the National Art Collections Fund in its attempts to secure masterpieces for Scotland. Many of these acquisitions are works by Scottish artists, for the Gallery continues to take very seriously its designated rôle as the national repository of the Scottish school. Acquisitions of the last ten years or so have included major pictures by Ramsay, Wilkie, Nasmyth and Dyce.

The display in the Gallery has also been immeasurably enriched by generous loans made to the collection over the years, some anonymously. One of the most important early Netherlandish paintings in the country, Hugo van der Goes's *The Trinity Altar-*

piece, has been on loan from the Royal Collection since 1931, while the superlative pictures from the collection of the Duke of Sutherland have been lent since 1945 and 1946 (for more information about the Sutherland loan see p. 17). This catalogue includes the Trinity altarpiece, the Sutherland pictures and the Torrie Collection Ruisdael on the basis of the longstanding nature of these loans.

From their inception the National Galleries have displayed and purchased 'modern' art and a gallery specifically devoted to this area of collecting was opened in August 1960 at Inverleith House, in the middle of the Royal Botanic Gardens. A need for expansion caused the gallery to move in 1983 to its current site in the former John Watson's School at Belford Road. The Scottish National Gallery of Modern Art is also shortly to gain a neighbouring building housing the Paolozzi Gift at the Dean Centre across the road. The National Galleries have also expanded in other areas, displaying some 80 pictures in the magnificent gallery in Paxton House in Berwickshire, about 60 miles southeast of Edinburgh, and also showing some 200 works in its new country house gallery 'outstation' in one of the architect William Adam's most renowned buildings, Duff House, in Banffshire. In keeping with its history, the National Gallery of Scotland has shown that it has remained true to the principles of its foundation as a 'temple for the Fine Arts' as Prince Albert predicted when the first stone was laid in 1850.

For further information on the history of the Gallery and the formation of its collections, reference should be made to the Gallery's publications: *Pictures for Scotland. The National Gallery of Scotland and its collection: a study of the changing attitude to painting since the 1820s* (Edinburgh 1972) and *The National Gallery of Scotland. An Architectural and Decorative History* (Edinburgh 1988). See too *The Concise Catalogue of the Scottish National Portrait Gallery* (Edinburgh 1990) and *The Concise Catalogue of the Scottish National Gallery of Modern Art* (Edinburgh 1993) for more information on the history of those collections.

LIST OF PRINCIPAL CURATORS, DIRECTORS AND KEEPERS OF THE NATIONAL GALLERY OF SCOTLAND

From the opening of the Gallery in 1859 until the National Gallery of Scotland Act of 1906, the head of the National Gallery was known as the 'Principal Curator and Keeper'. (The first of these was appointed in 1858 to prepare for the opening of the Gallery the following year.) The posts of Director and of Keeper did not come into force until April 1907. However, until 1967 the Keeper was not a full-time curatorial post at the National Gallery at the Mound (the Portrait Gallery rather than the National Gallery appears mainly to have been the post's remit). Keepers have therefore been listed from after 1967 only.

Principal Curators

1858–68	William B. Johnstone RSA
1868–77	James Drummond RSA
1877–82	Sir William Fettes Douglas PRSA
1882–94	Gourlay Steell RSA
1895–1907	Robert Gibb RSA

Directors

1907–30	Sir James L. Caw LLD, FSAScot.
1930–48	Sir Stanley Cursiter CBE, LLD, RSA, FRSE
1949–52	Sir Ellis K. Waterhouse CBE, FBA, D.Litt., MA
1952–70	David Baxandall BA, FMA
1970–77	Hugh Scrutton CBE, MA, FMA
1977–84	Colin Thompson CBE, D.Univ., FRSE, MA, FMA
1984–	Timothy Clifford BA, AMA, LLD, FRSA, FSAScot.

Keepers

1967–77	Colin Thompson CBE, D.Univ., FRSE, MA, FMA
1978–86	Hugh Macandrew MA
1987–	Michael Clarke BA, FRSA

THE DUKE OF SUTHERLAND LOAN

The majority of the pictures placed on loan at the National Gallery of Scotland by the Duke of Sutherland were originally acquired by the 3rd Duke of Bridgewater (1736–1803). Sixteen of them came from the collection of the Duc d'Orléans, and three of these had belonged to Queen Christina of Sweden (sold by her heir in 1692 to Prince Livio Odescalchi, and by his heir in 1721 to the Duc d'Orléans). In 1791 Louis Philippe Joseph, Duc d'Orléans ('Philippe Egalité'), sold his Italian and French pictures to Viscount Walchiers of Brussels. They were bought from him by François de Laborde de Méréville, who hoped to save them for the French nation but was forced to send them to England. They were sold in London in 1797–8 to Mr Bryan, who was acting for the Duke of Bridgewater, his nephew Earl Gower and the Earl of Carlisle (brother-in-law of Earl Gower). All the pictures were exhibited for sale at Bryan's Gallery and the Lyceum Gallery from 26 December 1798, but the majority were reserved for this syndicate of three.

At his death in 1803 the Duke of Bridgewater stipulated that most of his pictures, including his share of the Orléans collection, and Bridgewater House where most of them were hung, were made over with a life interest to his nephew, Earl Gower, but would eventually pass to his nephew's second son (since the first was to inherit Earl Gower's own estate and titles). Earl Gower inherited the title of Marquess of Stafford from his father and was later created 1st Duke of Sutherland. Both the Bridgewater and Stafford collections were housed together in the Stafford Gallery until Earl Gower's death in 1833. The titles of Marquess of Stafford and Duke of Sutherland were inherited by the eldest boy, George Granville Leveson Gower, but according to the will of the Duke of Bridgewater, it was the second son, Lord Francis, who inherited most of the Bridgewater collection. Lord Francis took the Duke of Bridgewater's family surname of Egerton and was made Earl of Ellesmere in 1846. The pictures passed by descent to the 5th Earl of Ellesmere who became the present and 6th Duke of Sutherland in 1963. (The dukedom is inherited through the male line and therefore reverted to the Ellesmeres when the 5th Duke died without a son.) It is by the Duke of Sutherland's generosity that the present loan was arranged with the Gallery in 1945 with a few more works being lent in 1946 (the loan was made before his inheritance of the dukedom and so is also often referred to as the Ellesmere loan). In 1984 the Gallery purchased four paintings by Private Treaty from the Ellesmere Trustees with a grant from the National Heritage Memorial Fund (Lotto NG 2418, Tintoretto NG 2419, Dou NG 2420, Steen NG 2421). The remaining twenty-six works on loan to the National Gallery of Scotland, which are all included in this catalogue, are listed here:

Gerard ter BORCH	*A Singing Practice*
DUTCH School	*An Old Lady Wearing a Ruff*
Attributed to Van DYCK	*Portrait of a Young Man*
Meindert HOBBEMA	*Landscape with a View of the Bergkerk, Deventer*
Nicolas POUSSIN	*Moses Striking the Rock*
Nicolas POUSSIN	*The Sacrament of Baptism*
Nicolas POUSSIN	*The Sacrament of Confirmation*
Nicolas POUSSIN	*The Sacrament of Marriage*
Nicolas POUSSIN	*The Sacrament of Penance*
Nicolas POUSSIN	*The Sacrament of Ordination*
Nicolas POUSSIN	*The Sacrament of the Holy Eucharist*
Nicolas POUSSIN	*The Sacrament of Extreme Unction*
RAPHAEL	*The Holy Family with a Palm Tree*
RAPHAEL	*The Bridgewater Madonna*
RAPHAEL and Studio	*The Madonna del Passeggio*
After RAPHAEL	*The Madonna with the Veil*
REMBRANDT	*Self-portrait, aged 51*
Studio of REMBRANDT	*A Young Woman with Flowers in her Hair*
Studio of REMBRANDT	*Hannah and Samuel*
Follower of REMBRANDT	*A Study of a Man's Head ('Portrait of a Jew')*
TINTORETTO	*Portrait of a Venetian*
TITIAN	*The Virgin and Child with St John the Baptist and an unidentified Male Saint*
TITIAN	*The Three Ages of Man*
TITIAN	*Venus Anadyomene*
TITIAN	*Diana and Actaeon*
TITIAN	*Diana and Callisto*

LIST OF ABBREVIATIONS USED IN THE CATALOGUE

c.	*circa*, about
fl.	*floruit*, flourished, was active
GMA	Scottish National Gallery of Modern Art
RAPFAS	Royal Association for the Promotion of Fine Arts of Scotland
RSA	Royal Scottish Academy
RI	Royal Institution
SNPG	Scottish National Portrait Gallery

ORGANISATION OF THE CATALOGUE

Works included

This catalogue is a checklist of every painting from every school in the collection of the National Gallery of Scotland. Also included for historical reasons are a few works on paper (usually in the medium of oil paint) which were originally accessioned as paintings. In all cases these works on paper are bonded onto another support, either board, panel or canvas. With these few exceptions all other works on paper are excluded from this catalogue as they are part of the Prints and Drawings collection.

In addition to those pictures on loan from the Duke of Sutherland, which were all placed on loan in 1945 and 1946, it has also been decided to include loans which have been on display in the Gallery for more than 50 years. These are Her Majesty the Queen's *The Trinity Altarpiece* by Hugo van der Goes (which was first shown in the Gallery in 1912 and then displayed on permanent loan from 1931) and the Torrie Collection's *The Banks of a River* by Jacob van Ruisdael (which has been in the Gallery since 1859).

The Catalogue Entries

The paintings are catalogued alphabetically by artist's name. When an artist is known by an alternative name this is given in brackets afterwards. Where there is more than one work by the same artist, these are listed in order of their acquisition.

A numerical list of acquisitions can be found on p. 393. A sample entry from the concise catalogue reads:

James DRUMMOND	*Artist's name (attribution)*
(1816–77) Scottish	*Artist's dates of birth and death and nationality*
The Porteous Mob	*Title of picture*
Oil on canvas: 123 x 123	*Medium, support and measurements*
Signed and dated 1855	*Artist's signature and date on work*
Transferred from RAPFAS 1897	*Method of acquisition and date when acquired*
NG 180	*National Gallery of Scotland accession number*

For guidance the following notes describe each category:

Attribution

The surname or name by which the artist is most commonly known is given in capitals. Works believed to be by the artist are listed first, works attributed to the artist follow, and works more loosely connected with the artist are listed afterwards. The hierarchy is as follows:

RUBENS	Painted by Rubens
Attributed to RUBENS	There is some uncertainty about the authorship of the painting due to style, iconography, subject or condition
Workshop/Studio of RUBENS	Painted by an unknown artist trained by Rubens or working in his studio, possibly with some participation by Rubens
Circle of RUBENS	By an artist whose work is closely related to that of Rubens but who did not work in Rubens's studio
Follower of RUBENS	Painted by someone strongly influenced by Rubens's work, sometimes of a later date
Style of RUBENS	Painted in the style of Rubens but may be of a later period
Imitator of RUBENS	Painted by someone trying to imitate the work of Rubens, may be of a later date
After RUBENS	Of a later date and painted in direct imitation of a known work by Rubens

Re-attributions

For this concise catalogue (as opposed to a school catalogue), it has been decided to change attributions only where new information has led to a consensus for alteration. In some cases only a school of painting is mentioned and an indication of a century, details which will be clarified in the school catalogues. All re-attributions made since previous catalogues are listed under their *new* attributions. A list of all re-attributions made since the publication of previous catalogues can be found on p. 404.

Artists' Dates

The dates of birth and death of the artists have been supplied where these are known. In some cases the following will appear:

c. 1650 – *c.* 1720	The artist was born in about 1650 and died in about 1720
c. 1650–1720	The artist was born in about 1650 and died in 1720
1650/58–1720	The artist was born some time between 1650 and 1658
active 1650	The artist was known to be working in and around this year

Nationality

The nationality of the artists has been stated but in a few cases dual nationality has been given, usually when an artist was born in one country but spent most of his working life in another.

A distinction is made in this catalogue between Netherlandish, Dutch and Flemish schools. *Netherlandish* is used for artists from both the northern and southern Netherlands prior to the Union of Utrecht in 1579. Roughly after this date *Dutch* is used to distinguish artists from the northern Netherlands (which seceded to become the United Provinces) from those in the southern Netherlands, here called *Flemish*.

Titles

Titles given in brackets are traditional titles that may not be original and may be misleading. Where the work is a portrait, dates of the sitter are given when known. Where a listed work relates directly to another in this collection (for instance an oil study for a picture), this is cross-referenced within the text.

Medium and Support

In a few works, it has not been possible to determine if oil paint or tempera was used and in these cases only the support is listed. Canvas, metal, ivory or panel is mentioned but in the case of the latter, the type of wood is not specified.

Measurements

All measurements are given in centimetres, height before width. The most recent measurement has always been used and any difference from previous catalogues indicates that the work has been re-measured since those publications. Where a work is incomplete, cut-down or is a fragment this has been noted.

Signatures and Inscriptions

All signatures and inscriptions are on the front of the work unless otherwise stated. Transcriptions of signatures and inscriptions are not given here but it is noted if signatures are in the form of a monogram or cipher. Where the entry cites 'With signature' or 'With inscription', it is suspected that these may not be autograph (i.e. by the artist of the picture) but by another, sometimes later, hand.

Dated Works

Dates of pictures are only listed where these appear on the work itself. When abbreviated on the work (such as '98) the date has been cited in full (i.e. 1898) for clarity. Square brackets are used when a digit is indistinct or missing.

Method and Date of Acquisition

Bequests are usually quoted in the year of the death of the donor but occasionally the works were not received until a number of years afterwards, for instance where someone was given a life-interest in the estate. In these cases the year of the original bequest is given (when known), as well as the year the work was finally received by the Gallery.

As the history of the Gallery shows (pp. 9–15), many works were transferred from the Royal Institution, the Royal Scottish Academy and other sources. The date of original acquisition by the other institution has been given where it is known, as well as the date of transfer.

Illustrations

Unlike previous publications, this catalogue illustrates every work, even where the state of condition is poor. Where works have painting on both sides, this is stated in the entry and the reverse is also illustrated. Though not all works have been re-photographed for the catalogue, any picture which has been restored is shown in the state of its most recent conservation.

CATALOGUE

William AIKMAN
(1682–1732) Scottish
Self-portrait
Oil on canvas: 73.6 x 62.2
Presented to the RSA by James T. Gibson-Craig
1859; transferred and presented 1910
NG 167

Cosmo ALEXANDER
(1724–72) Scottish
Adrian Hope of Amsterdam (1709–81)
Oil on canvas: 77.5 x 64
Signed and dated 1763
Purchased 1937
NG 1882

Cosmo ALEXANDER
(1724–72) Scottish
James Duff of Corsindae (1678–1762)
Oil on canvas: 77 x 64.5
Inscribed, signed and dated 1760
Presented by Miss Henrietta Tayler 1944
NG 2022

John ALEXANDER
(1686– *c.* 1766) Scottish
The Rape of Proserpine
Oil on canvas: 71.1 x 80.7
Inscribed, signed and dated 1720
Purchased 1932
NG 1784

John ALEXANDER
(1686– *c.* 1766) Scottish
Portrait of an Old Lady, possibly Margaret Gordon, Mrs Alexander Duff of Braco
Oil on canvas: 76.2 x 63.5
Reverse: with inscription and date 1736
Purchased 1934
NG 1798

Robert ALEXANDER
(1840–1923) Scottish
The Happy Mother
Oil on canvas: 81.5 x 116.3
Signed and dated 1887
Bequest of Mrs Annie Ogilvie Cooper 1925
NG 1648

David ALLAN
(1744–96) Scottish
*Mrs James Tassie, probably Ann
Harker (1730–90)*
Oil on canvas: 75.8 x 63.2
Bequest of William Tassie 1860
NG 415

David ALLAN
(1744–96) Scottish
The Origin of Painting ('The Maid of Corinth')
Oil on panel: 38.7 x 31 (oval)
Reverse: signed and dated 1775
Presented by Mrs Byres of Tonley 1874
NG 612

David ALLAN
(1744–96) Scottish
The Uncultivated Genius
Oil on copper: 23.9 x 18.5
Reverse: inscribed, signed with initials
and dated 1775
Purchased 1950
NG 2126

David ALLAN
(1744–96) Scottish
Sir John Halkett of Pitfirrane, 4th Bart (1720–93),
Mary Hamilton, Lady Halkett and their Family
Oil on canvas: 153 x 239.5
Signed and dated 1781
Bequest of Miss Madeline Halkett
of Pitfirrane 1951
NG 2157

David ALLAN
(1744–96) Scottish
The Continence of Scipio
Oil on canvas: 161 x 137
Reverse: inscribed, signed and dated 1774
Purchased 1962
NG 2256

David ALLAN
(1744–96) Scottish
The Connoisseurs: John Caw (died 1784),
John Bonar (1747–1807) and James Bruce
Oil on canvas: 87.5 x 101.9
Reverse: inscribed, signed and dated 1783
Purchased 1963
NG 2260

David ALLAN
(1744–96) Scottish
James Colvin
Oil on canvas: 37.5 x 30.2
Reverse: inscribed and dated 1783
Presented by Miss Elsie N. Adam 1967
NG 2292

Sir William ALLAN
(1782–1850) Scottish
The Black Dwarf
Oil on panel: 33.2 x 44.5
Signed (indistinctly)
Commissioned by the RI in 1827; transferred 1859
NG 172

Sir William ALLAN
(1782–1850) Scottish
The Murder of David Rizzio
Oil on panel: 102.5 x 163.3
Presented by the 3rd Baron Strathcona
and Mount Royal 1927
NG 1677

Sir William ALLAN
(1782–1850) Scottish
A Study for 'The Murder of David Rizzio'
(NG 1677)
Oil on panel: 41.3 x 70.2
Purchased 1979
NG 2380

Sir William ALLAN
(1782–1850) Scottish
The Slave Market, Constantinople
Oil on panel: 129 x 198
Signed and dated 1838
Purchased 1980
NG 2400

Attributed to Giuliano AMIDEI
(active 1446 – died 1496) Italian
The Death of St Ephraim
Panel: 34 x 43.5 (irregular fragment;
made up to a rectangle)
Purchased 1921
NG 1528

Attributed to APOLLONIO di Giovanni
(1415/17–1465) Italian
The Triumphs of Love and Chastity
Tempera and gold on panel: 44 x 143
Bequest of the 11th Marquess of Lothian 1941
NG 1940

Workshop of APOLLONIO di Giovanni
(1415/17–1465) Italian
The Rape of the Sabines
Tempera and gold on panel: 39.3 x 61.5 (fragment)
Purchased 1942
NG 1974

James ARCHER
(1822–1904) Scottish
Emelye
Oil on millboard: 35.5 x 23.9
Signed in monogram
Bequest of Alexander F. Roberts 1929
NG 1729

James ARCHER
(1822–1904) Scottish
Summertime, Gloucestershire
Oil on canvas: 76.4 x 106
Purchased with the aid of the Florence Clark
Bequest Fund for the purchase of Scottish Art 1979
NG 2381

After Hans ASPER
(1499–1571) Swiss
Huldrych Zwingli (1484–1531)
Oil on panel: 25.5 x 19
Bequest of the 11th Marquess of Lothian 1941
NG 1927

Hendrick AVERCAMP
(1585–1634) Dutch
Winter Landscape
Oil on copper: 28.6 x 42.2
Signed in monogram
Bequest of David Laing 1879
NG 647

BACCHIACCA (Francesco Ubertini)
(1494–1557) Italian
Moses Striking the Rock
Oil and gold on panel: 100 x 80
Purchased 1967
NG 2291

Ludolf BACKHUYZEN
(1630/31–1708) Dutch
Shipping in a Choppy Sea
Oil on canvas: 59 x 82.6 (painted area)
Signed
Bequest of Miss Alice Anne White 1941
NG 1946

Emilius Ditlev BAERENTZEN
(1799–1868) Danish
The Winther Family
Oil on canvas: 70.5 x 65.5
Signed and dated 1827
Purchased with the aid of the Patrons
of the National Galleries of Scotland
and the National Art Collections Fund 1987
NG 2451

Jacopo BASSANO (Jacopo dal Ponte)
(*c.* 1510–92) Italian
The Adoration of the Kings
Oil on canvas: 183 x 235
Purchased by the RSA 1856; transferred
and presented 1910
NG 100

Studio of Jacopo BASSANO (Jacopo dal Ponte)
(*c.* 1510–92) Italian
*Christ Driving the Moneychangers
from the Temple*
Oil on canvas: 168 x 230.5
Purchased by the RI 1826; transferred 1859
NG 4

Studio of Jacopo BASSANO (Jacopo dal Ponte)
(*c.* 1510–92) Italian
The Adoration of the Shepherds
Oil on canvas: 97.5 x 126
Bequest of Mrs Nisbet Hamilton Ogilvy
of Biel 1921
NG 1511

Studio of Jacopo BASSANO (Jacopo dal Ponte)
(*c.* 1510–92) Italian
The Virgin and Child with St John the Baptist and a Donor
Oil on canvas: 76.2 x 77
Bequest of Sir Claude Phillips 1924
NG 1635

After Jacopo BASSANO (Jacopo dal Ponte)
(*c.* 1510–92) Italian
St Francis Kneeling before the Virgin and Child
Oil on canvas: 35.5 x 30.2
Bequest of Sir Claude Phillips 1924
NG 1636

Jules BASTIEN-LEPAGE
(1848–84) French
Pas Mèche (Nothing Doing)
Oil on canvas: 132.1 x 89.5
Inscribed, signed and dated 1882
Purchased 1913
NG 1133

Pompeo Girolamo BATONI
(1708–87) Italian
Princess Cecilia Mahony Giustiniani (1741–89)
Oil on canvas: 73.7 x 60.7
Inscribed, signed and dated 1785
Purchased with the aid of the
National Art Collections Fund 1978
NG 2369

Pompeo Girolamo BATONI
(1708–87) Italian
*Alexander Gordon, 4th Duke of Gordon
(1743–1827)*
Oil on canvas: 292 x 192
Inscribed, signed and dated 1764
Purchased by Private Treaty with the aid
of the National Heritage Memorial Fund
and the National Art Collections Fund 1994
NG 2589

After Giovanni BELLINI
(active 1459 – died 1516) Italian
The Feast of the Gods
Oil on canvas: 174 x 190.5
Presented by Sir Charles Eastlake 1863
NG 458

Ambrosius BENSON
(active 1519 – died 1550) Netherlandish
The Virgin and Child with St Anne
Oil on panel: 80.7 x 59.1 (ogee top)
Purchased 1945
NG 2024

Jean-Victor BERTIN
(1767–1842) French
Classical Landscape
Oil on canvas: 63.5 x 87
Signed and dated 'an VIII' [1800]
Purchased 1988
NG 2465

Joseph BIDAULD
(1758–1846) French
*The Heights of Sannois seen from the Plain
of Argenteuil*
Oil on paper laid on canvas: 22 x 47.7
Purchased 1987
NG 2446

Joseph BIDAULD
(1758–1846) French
An Alley of Trees in a Park
Oil on canvas: 40 x 32
Purchased 1995
NG 2642

Pieter van BLOEMEN
(1657–1720) Flemish
Landscape with a Herdsman and Animals in front of the Baths of Diocletian, Rome
Oil on canvas: 48.5 x 63.5 (painted area)
Bequest of Mrs Mary Veitch to the RSA 1875; transferred and presented 1910
NG 1014

Henry BONE
(1755–1834) English
Sir Francis Drake (c. 1540–96)
(after English School, 16th century, formerly ascribed to Jan van Belkamp)
Enamel on copper: 13 x 10.3
Signed and dated 1814
Reverse: with inscription
Bequest of Dr Donald Fraser 1880
NG 660

Henry BONE
(1755–1834) English
*An Old Woman and a Boy with a Lighted Candle
(after Rubens)*
Enamel on copper: 20.3 x 17.5
Reverse: with inscription
Bequest of Dr Donald Fraser 1880
NG 661

Studio of BONIFAZIO Veronese
(Bonifazio de' Pitati)
(1487–1553) Italian
The Last Supper
Oil on canvas: 144.5 x 278.5
Purchased by the RI 1849; transferred 1859
NG 9

Richard Parkes BONINGTON
(1802–28) English
Landscape with Mountains
Oil on millboard: 25.1 x 33
Purchased 1910
NG 1017

Richard Parkes BONINGTON
(1802–28) English
Venice: The Grand Canal
Oil on paper laid on canvas: 25.4 x 32.5
Bequest of Lady Binning 1952
NG 2164

Richard Parkes BONINGTON
(1802–28) English
An Estuary with a Sailing Boat
Oil on millboard: 22.9 x 35.3
Bequest of Lady Binning 1952
NG 2165

William BONNAR
(1800–53) Scottish
Self-portrait
Oil on panel: 33 x 26.1
Presented by Thomas Bonnar 1879
NG 642

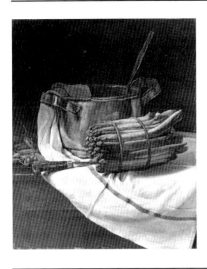

François BONVIN
(1817–87) French
Still Life with Asparagus
Oil on canvas: 61.6 x 50.3
Signed and dated 1881
Purchased 1990
NG 2524

Gerard ter BORCH
(1617–81) Dutch
A Singing Practice
Oil on canvas: 73.8 x 79.6
Lent by the Duke of Sutherland 1945

Paris BORDON
(1500–71) Italian
Venetian Women at their Toilet
Oil on canvas: 97 x 141
Signed
Purchased by the RI 1830; transferred 1859
NG 10

Paris BORDON
(1500–71) Italian
The Rest on the Return from Egypt
Oil on canvas: 104 x 140.8
Accepted in lieu of tax with a contribution from
Gallery funds 1996
NG 2651

Orazio BORGIANNI
(1577/78–1616) Italian
St Christopher
Oil on canvas: 104 x 78
Presented to the RSA by Sir John Watson Gordon
1850; transferred and presented 1910
NG 48

After Orazio BORGIANNI
(1577/78–1616) Italian
St Christopher
Oil on canvas: 99 x 73.8
Purchased by the RI 1830; transferred 1859
NG 20

Johannes BOSBOOM
(1817–91) Dutch
The Preacher
Oil on panel: 28.6 x 42.5
Signed
Bequest of Dr John Kirkhope 1920
NG 1468

Johannes BOSBOOM
(1817–91) Dutch
The Interior of Alkmaar Church
Oil on panel: 18.5 x 14.6
Signed
Bequest of Dr John Kirkhope 1920
NG 1469

Jan BOTH
(*c.* 1615–52) Dutch
Landscape
Oil on panel: 44.5 x 54
Bequest of Patrick Shaw 1903
NG 912

Jan BOTH
(c. 1615–52) Dutch
Landscape
Oil on copper: 49.6 x 65.3
Bequest of Patrick Shaw 1903
NG 913

Attributed to Jan BOTH
(c. 1615–52) Dutch
Landscape
Oil on canvas: 49.9 x 73.2
Purchased by the RI 1831; transferred 1859
NG 13

Studio of Sandro BOTTICELLI
(c. 1445–1510) Italian
*The Virgin and St John the Baptist
Adoring the Infant Christ*
Panel: 46.6 x 41.6
Purchased 1921
NG 1536

Circle of Sandro BOTTICELLI
(*c.* 1445–1510) Italian
St John the Baptist
Panel: 35 x 13.3
Bequest of Lord Carmichael of Skirling;
received 1948
NG 2099

After Sandro BOTTICELLI
(*c.* 1445–1510) Italian
Portrait of a Youth
Panel: 55 x 40.3
Purchased with the aid of the Cowan Smith
Bequest Fund 1933
NG 1792

François BOUCHER
(1703–70) French
A Pastoral Scene ('L'Offrande à la Villageoise')
Oil on canvas: 231.5 x 91 (painted area)
Signed and dated 1761
Purchased 1986
NG 2440

François BOUCHER
(1703–70) French
A Pastoral Scene ('La Jardinière Endormie')
Oil on canvas: 232 x 91 (painted area)
Signed and dated 1762
Purchased 1986
NG 2441

François BOUCHER
(1703–70) French
A Pastoral Scene ('L'Aimable Pastorale')
Oil on canvas: 231.5 x 91 (painted area)
Signed and dated 1762
Purchased 1986
NG 2442

Attributed to François BOUCHER
(1703–70) French
Madame de Pompadour
(Jeanne-Antoinette Poisson, 1721–64)
Oil on canvas: 37.9 x 46.3
Bequest of Lady Murray of Henderland 1861
NG 429

Attributed to François BOUCHER
(1703–70) French
The Assumption of the Virgin
Oil on canvas: 127 x 73.5
Bequest of R. T. G. Paterson 1955
NG 2179

Eugène BOUDIN
(1824–98) French
The Port of Bordeaux
Oil on canvas: 40 x 65.4
Inscribed, signed and dated 1874
Presented by George R. MacDougall 1912
NG 1072

Eugène BOUDIN
(1824–98) French
Washerwomen on the Banks of the Touques
Oil on panel: 26.7 x 41
Signed and dated 1894
Bequest of Alastair Russell MacWilliam 1977
NG 2349

Eugène BOUDIN
(1824–98) French
Kerhor: Fisherwomen Resting
Oil on panel: 23.8 x 41.2
Signed and dated 1871
Bequest of Dr Robert A. Lillie 1977
NG 2350

Eugène BOUDIN
(1824–98) French
A Fishing Boat, Trouville
Oil on panel: 27.1 x 21.3
Signed
Bequest of Dr Robert A. Lillie 1977
NG 2351

Eugène BOUDIN
(1824–98) French
Trouville Harbour
Oil on panel: 30.7 x 57.6
Inscribed, signed and dated 1873
Bequest of Agnes Anderson; received from the
estate of her daughter Mrs Jessie B. Agnew 1979
NG 2371

Eugène BOUDIN
(1824–98) French
The Beach at Trouville
Oil on panel: 13.7 x 23.4
Signed and dated 1884
Bequest of Agnes Anderson; received from the
estate of her daughter Mrs Jessie B. Agnew 1979
NG 2372

Eugène BOUDIN
(1824–98) French
Villefranche Harbour
Oil on canvas: 46 x 65
Inscribed, signed and dated 1892
Bequest of Agnes Anderson; received from the
estate of her daughter Mrs Jessie B. Agnew 1979
NG 2373

Eugène BOUDIN
(1824–98) French
The Bridge over the Touques at Deauville
Oil on canvas: 36.3 x 58.5
Inscribed, signed and dated 1895
Presented by Mrs Isabel M. Traill 1979
NG 2392

Eugène BOUDIN
(1824–98) French
Golfe-Juan
Oil on canvas: 27 x 41
Inscribed, signed and dated 1893
Presented by J. Percival Agnew 1981
NG 2406

Attributed to Eugène BOUDIN
(1824–98) French
Venice: View from the Giudecca
Oil on canvas: 36 x 55
With signature
Bequest of Agnes Anderson; received from the
estate of her daughter Mrs Jessie B. Agnew 1979
NG 2374

Samuel BOUGH
(1822–78) English/Scottish
Royal Volunteer Review, 7 August 1860
Oil on canvas: 118.1 x 179
Signed and dated 1860
Presented by Charles T. Combe 1887
NG 801

Samuel BOUGH
(1822–78) English/Scottish
An English Canal Scene
Oil on millboard: 30.7 x 45.9
Presented by David B. Anderson 1889
NG 819

Samuel BOUGH
(1822–78) English/Scottish
Off St Andrews
Oil on canvas: 36.2 x 45.8
Signed and dated 1856
Bequest of Dr John Kirkhope 1920
NG 1475

Samuel BOUGH
(1822–78) English/Scottish
The Solway at Port Carlisle
Oil on panel: 25.5 x 32.5
Signed
Bequest of Dr John Kirkhope 1920
NG 1476

Samuel BOUGH
(1822–78) English/Scottish
Berwick-on-Tweed
Oil on panel: 20.1 x 29.2
Signed
Reverse: inscribed
Bequest of Miss Ida M. Hayward 1950
NG 2121

Jan de BRAIJ (de BRAY)
(1626/27–1697) Dutch
Portrait of a Man
Oil on panel: 23.5 x 17.4 (oval)
Inscribed, signed and dated 1662
Bequest of Mrs Nisbet Hamilton Ogilvy
of Biel 1921
NG 1500

Jan de BRAIJ (de BRAY)
(1626/27–1697) Dutch
Portrait of a Woman
Oil on panel: 23.5 x 17.4 (oval)
Inscribed, signed and dated 1663
Bequest of Mrs Nisbet Hamilton Ogilvy
of Biel 1921
NG 1501

Jan de BRAIJ (de BRAY)
(1626/27–1697) Dutch
Portrait of a Boy
Oil on panel: 21.2 x 15.2 (oval)
Inscribed, signed and dated 1662
Bequest of Mrs Nisbet Hamilton Ogilvy
of Biel 1921
NG 1502

Jan de BRAIJ (de BRAY)
(1626/27–1697) Dutch
Portrait of a Boy
Oil on panel: 21.5 x 15.8 (oval)
Inscribed, signed and dated 1663
Bequest of Mrs Nisbet Hamilton Ogilvy
of Biel 1921
NG 1503

Paul BRIL
(1553/54–1626) Flemish
Fantastic Landscape
Oil on copper: 21.3 x 29.2
Inscribed, signed and dated 1598
Bequest of Mrs Nisbet Hamilton Ogilvy
of Biel 1921
NG 1492

BRITISH School
(17th century)
Portrait of a Young Man
Oil on canvas: 78.1 x 61.7
Purchased 1934
NG 1824

After BRONZINO (Agnolo di Cosimo)
(1503–72) Italian
Garzia or Giovanni de' Medici
Oil on canvas: 26.5 x 19.5
Bequest of the 11th Marquess of Lothian 1941
NG 1943

Robert BROUGH
(1872–1905) Scottish
William Dallas Ross (died 1931)
Oil on canvas: 73.5 x 59
Signed and dated 1893
Presented by William Dallas Ross 1907
NG 938

Follower of Hendrick ter BRUGGHEN
(c. 1588–1629) Dutch
The Beheading of St John the Baptist
Oil on canvas: 168 x 218
Presented by James S. Wardrop
for the future National Gallery 1850
NG 28

John BURNET
(1784–1868) Scottish
An Oyster-cellar in Leith
Oil on panel: 29.5 x 35.3
Purchased 1931
NG 1759

Robert BURNS
(1869–1941) Scottish
Diana and her Nymphs
Canvas: 198.1 x 198.1
Purchased 1987
NG 2450

Robert BURNS
(1869–1941) Scottish
A Girl with a Hawk
Canvas: 76.5 x 64.2
Signed and dated 1901
Purchased 1989
NG 2490

Alexander Hohenlohe BURR
(1835–99) Scottish
The Night Stall
Oil on canvas: 54 x 48.8
Signed in monogram and dated 1860
Purchased 1910
NG 1000

John BURR
(1831–93) Scottish
Grandfather's Return
Oil on canvas: 24.8 x 28.6
Purchased 1910
NG 1001

Studio of Bernardino BUTINONE
(active 1484 – died 1507) Italian
Christ Disputing with the Doctors
Panel: 25.1 x 22.3
Purchased 1930
NG 1746

James CADENHEAD
(1858–1927) Scottish
A Highland Pastoral
Oil on canvas: 74.3 x 102.3
Signed in monogram
Presented by Miss Grace H. Findlay 1948
NG 2106

Abraham van CALRAET
(1642–1722) Dutch
The Start
Oil on panel: 32 x 47 (painted area)
Signed with initials
Bequest of Mrs Nisbet Hamilton Ogilvy
of Biel 1921
NG 1493

Denys CALVAERT
(1540–1619) Flemish/Italian
*The Holy Family with the Infant St John the
Baptist in a Landscape*
Oil on copper: 42 x 32
Purchased with the aid of the Patrons of
the National Galleries of Scotland
and the National Art Collections Fund 1987
NG 2447

Luca CAMBIASO
(1527–85) Italian
*The Holy Family with the Infant St John
the Baptist*
Oil on canvas: 143 x 106.7
Purchased by the RI 1830; transferred 1859
NG 18

Adam CAMERARIUS
(active *c.* 1645–65) Dutch
A Young Man in a Fur Cap
Oil on canvas: 78.5 x 66
Signed and dated 1649
Purchased by the RI 1840; transferred 1859
NG 8

Sir David Young CAMERON
(1865–1945) Scottish
Glencaple
Oil on canvas: 76.2 x 102.2
Signed
Bequest of Robert Younger,
Baron Blanesburgh 1947
NG 2079

Sir David Young CAMERON
(1865–1945) Scottish
Hill of the Winds
Oil on canvas: 116.8 x 132.7
Signed
Bequest of Robert Younger,
Baron Blanesburgh 1947
NG 2080

Sir David Young CAMERON
(1865–1945) Scottish
En Provence
Oil on canvas: 67.3 x 83.2
Signed
Bequest of Robert Younger,
Baron Blanesburgh 1947
NG 2081

Sir David Young CAMERON
(1865–1945) Scottish
La rue Annette
Oil on canvas: 51 x 35.5
Signed
Bequest of Sir Alexander Maitland 1965
NG 2383

Sir David Young CAMERON
(1865–1945) Scottish
Ben Ledi: Late Autumn
Oil on canvas: 35.6 x 36
Signed
Bequest of Mrs Isabel M. Traill 1986
NG 2443

Sir David Young CAMERON
(1865–1945) Scottish
Rocks and Ruins
Oil on canvas: 51 x 46
Signed with initials
Reverse: with inscription and date 1913
Bequest of Mr and Mrs G. D. Robinson
through the National Art Collections Fund 1988
NG 2455

Hugh CAMERON
(1835–1918) Scottish
Going to the Hay
Oil on canvas: 57.2 x 42.5
Signed and dated 1858
Presented by James T. Gibson-Craig 1879
NG 652

Hugh CAMERON
(1835–1918) Scottish
A Toiler of the Hills
Oil on canvas: 75.6 x 95.9
Signed and dated 1911
Purchased 1920
NG 1444

Hugh CAMERON
(1835–1918) Scottish
A Lonely Life
Oil on canvas: 84.5 x 63.5
Signed
Purchased 1928
NG 1717

Hugh CAMERON
(1835–1918) Scottish
A Girl Sewing ('Quiet Work')
Oil on canvas: 46.4 x 33.7
Signed
Bequest of Alexander F. Roberts 1929
NG 1730

Hugh CAMERON
(1835–1918) Scottish
Buttercups and Daisies (The Artist's Daughter)
Oil on canvas: 68 x 47.6
Signed
Presented by Miss M. Kerr Cameron 1931
NG 1763

Hugh CAMERON
(1835–1918) Scottish
A Study for 'A Toiler of the Hills' (NG 1444)
Oil on canvas: 35.5 x 50
Presented by Miss M. Kerr Cameron 1931
NG 1764

Hugh CAMERON
(1835–1918) Scottish
Youth's Bright Sunny Day
Oil on canvas: 63.5 x 108.2
Signed
Bequest of John Mackie Croall 1952
NG 2162

Follower of CANALETTO (Giovanni Antonio Canal)
(1697–1768) Italian
The Grand Canal, Venice
Oil on canvas: 65 x 83.8
Purchased by the RI 1831; transferred 1859
NG 17

Follower of CANALETTO (Giovanni Antonio Canal)
(1697–1768) Italian
*The Grand Canal, Santa Lucia
and the Church of the Scalzi, Venice*
Oil on canvas: 37.1 x 55.3
Bequest of Miss Margaret J. Leadbetter 1944
NG 2014

Simone CANTARINI
(1612–48) Italian
The Holy Trinity
Oil on canvas: 190 x 126 (unfinished)
Presented to the RI by Edward Cruickshank 1844;
transferred 1859
NG 42

Vicente CARDUCHO (Vincenzo Carducci)
(1576–1638) Spanish
The Dream of St Hugh, Bishop of Grenoble
Oil on canvas: 57 x 45.5
Presented by Andrew Coventry 1863
NG 459

CARIANI (Giovanni Busi)
(*c.* 1485 – after 1547) Italian
Portrait of a Young Woman as St Agatha
Oil on canvas: 69 x 58
Purchased with the aid of the National Art
Collections Fund 1989
NG 2494

Alexander CARSE
(c. 1770–1843) Scottish
The New Web
Oil on canvas: 47.3 x 62.5
Presented by John Ritchie Findlay 1885
NG 780

Alexander CARSE
(c. 1770–1843) Scottish
A Brawl Outside an Ale House
Oil on canvas: 43.2 x 53.4
Signed and dated 1822
Purchased 1935
NG 1828

Follower of Andrea del CASTAGNO
(c. 1419–57) Italian
The Last Supper
Panel: 29.9 x 36.2
Purchased 1917
NG 1210

Bernardo CASTELLO
(1557–1629) Italian
The Adoration of the Shepherds
Oil on canvas: 45.7 x 34.9
Purchased by the RI 1830; transferred 1859
NG 56

Attributed to Vincenzo CATENA
(*c.* 1480–1531) Italian
Portrait of a Venetian Lady
Panel: 35 x 27
Purchased 1927
NG 1675

CERANO (Giovanni Battista Crespi)
(*c.* 1575–1632) Italian
The Head of St Francis in Ecstasy
Oil on panel: 41 x 35.5
Presented by Colonel J. A. Stirling of Cauldhame
and Kippendavie 1950
NG 2129

Paul CÉZANNE
(1839–1906) French
The Big Trees
Oil on canvas: 81 x 65
Presented by Mrs Anne F. Kessler 1958;
received after her death 1983
NG 2206

Paul CÉZANNE
(1839–1906) French
Montagne Sainte-Victoire
Oil on canvas: 55 x 65.4
Presented by Sir Alexander Maitland in memory
of his wife Rosalind 1960
NG 2236

Sir George CHALMERS
(c. 1720–91) Scottish
Portrait of an Old Lady
Oil on canvas: 76.2 x 63.5
Signed and dated 1769
Bequest of Miss Ella R. Christie 1949
NG 2113

Sir George CHALMERS
(c. 1720–91) Scottish
A Shepherdess Spied upon in a Landscape
Oil on canvas: 127 x 101.5
Signed and dated 1760
Purchased 1989
NG 2493

George Paul CHALMERS
(1833–78) Scottish
The Legend
Oil on canvas: 103 x 153
Purchased by RAPFAS 1878; transferred 1897
NG 657

George Paul CHALMERS
(1833–78) Scottish
A Quiet Cup
Oil on panel: 29.9 x 24.8
Purchased 1905
NG 924

George Paul CHALMERS
(1833–78) Scottish
Modesty
Oil on canvas: 65 x 39.3
Signed
Bequest of Dr John Kirkhope 1920
NG 1477

George Paul CHALMERS
(1833–78) Scottish
The Tired Devotee
Oil on canvas: 26.7 x 22.6
Signed and dated 1865
Bequest of Dr John Kirkhope 1920
NG 1478

George Paul CHALMERS
(1833–78) Scottish
The Eagle's Nest, Skye
Oil on canvas: 64.8 x 95.3
Signed
Purchased 1924
NG 1629

George Paul CHALMERS
(1833–78) Scottish
An Old Woman
Oil on canvas: 41.9 x 34.3
Signed
Bequest of Sir Andrew T. Taylor 1938
NG 1891

Jean-Siméon CHARDIN
(1699–1779) French
Still Life: The Kitchen Table
Oil on canvas: 40.6 x 32.4
Signed
Purchased 1908
NG 959

Jean-Siméon CHARDIN
(1699–1779) French
A Vase of Flowers
Oil on canvas: 45.2 x 37.1
Purchased 1937
NG 1883

James CHARLES
(1851–1906) English
A Cornfield near Wooler
Oil on canvas: 49.6 x 77.5
Signed in monogram
Presented by Sir Thomas Gibson Carmichael 1907
NG 942

George CHINNERY
(1774–1852) English
Self-portrait
Oil on canvas: 40.6 x 33
Purchased 1934; transferred from the SNPG 1969
NG 2303

Alexander CHRISTIE
(1807–60) Scottish
An Incident in the Great Plague of London
Oil on panel: 91.5 x 69.9
Presented by James T. Gibson-Craig 1870
NG 578

James Elder CHRISTIE
(1847–1914) Scottish
The Pied Piper of Hamelin
Oil on canvas: 69.5 x 98
Signed and dated 1881
Purchased 1919
NG 1231

Frederic Edwin CHURCH
(1826–1900) American
Niagara Falls from the American Side
Oil on canvas: 257.5 x 227.3
Signed and dated 1867
Presented by John S. Kennedy 1887
NG 799

Giovanni Battista CIMA da Conegliano
(*c.* 1459– *c.* 1517) Italian
The Virgin and Child with St Andrew and St Peter
Oil on panel: 55.6 x 47.2 (unfinished)
Presented by Miss Margaret Peter Dove 1915
NG 1190

CLAUDE LORRAIN (Claude Gellée)
(1600–82) French
Landscape with Apollo and the Muses
Oil on canvas: 186 x 290
Inscribed, signed and dated 1652
Purchased with the aid of the National Art
Collections Fund and a Treasury Grant 1960
NG 2240

Follower of CLAUDE LORRAIN (Claude Gellée)
(1600–82) French
Landscape with a Bridge
Oil on canvas: 63.2 x 78 (painted area)
Purchased 1908
NG 962

Sir George CLAUSEN
(1852–1944) English
Frieda
Oil on canvas: 45.7 x 35.6
Signed
Reverse: inscribed and dated 1920
Bequest of Sir David Young Cameron 1945
NG 2046

Sir George CLAUSEN
(1852–1944) English
The Stars Coming Out
Oil on canvas: 50.8 x 61.4
Signed and dated 1912
Reverse: inscribed
Bequest of Edward A. C. MacCurdy 1956;
received 1976
NG 2340

Joos van CLEVE
(active 1511 – died 1540/41) Netherlandish
Triptych. Centre: *The Deposition from the Cross.*
Left wing: *St John the Baptist with a Donor.*
Right wing: *St Margaret with a Donatrix*
Oil on panel: 106.7 x 71.1 (centre);
109.2 x 31.8 (wings)
Purchased 1920
NG 1252

Follower of Joos van CLEVE
(active 1511 – died 1540/41) Netherlandish
The Virgin and Child
Oil on panel: 36.2 x 24.1
Bequest of Mrs E. M. C. Thompson 1927
NG 1678

Attributed to François CLOUET
(c. 1510–72) French
Portrait of a Man, called the Duc d'Alençon
Oil on panel: 35.9 x 26
Accepted in lieu of tax 1984
NG 2426

Jean CLOUET
(c. 1485/90– c. 1540/41) French
Madame de Canaples (Marie d'Assigny, 1502–58)
Oil on panel: 36 x 28.5
Bequest of the 11th Marquess of Lothian 1941
NG 1930

John CONSTABLE
(1776–1837) English
On the Stour
Reverse: *Study of Cows* (see next item)
Oil on millboard: 20.3 x 23.5
Presented by Lady Binning 1918
NG 1219

John CONSTABLE
(1776–1837) English
Study of Cows
Reverse of NG 1219

John CONSTABLE
(1776–1837) English
The Vale of Dedham
Oil on canvas: 144.5 x 122
Purchased with the aid of the National Art
Collections Fund 1944
NG 2016

After John CONSTABLE
(1776–1837) English
Noon (Hampstead Heath)
Oil on canvas: 33.7 x 55.3
Bequest of Lady Binning 1952
NG 2163

Jan Daemen COOL
(1584–1660) Dutch
A Dutch Family Group (Portrait of Two Boys)
Oil on panel: 108 x 83.2 (cut down from NG 2259)
Inscribed
Purchased 1891
NG 824

Jan Daemen COOL
(1584–1660) Dutch
*A Dutch Family Group (Portrait of a Man,
Woman and Two Girls)*
Oil on panel: 133.4 x 115.6 (cut down)
Inscribed and dated 1633
Purchased 1963
NG 2259

Camille COROT
(1796–1875) French
Landscape at Coubron
Oil on canvas: 40 x 54.5
Signed
Bequest of Hugh A. Laird 1911
NG 1037

Camille COROT
(1796–1875) French
A Man Scything by a Willow Grove, Artois
Oil on canvas: 33.4 x 53.7
Signed
Bequest of Hugh A. Laird 1911
NG 1038

Camille COROT
(1796–1875) French
The Goatherd
Oil on canvas: 61.5 x 50
Signed
Bequest of Dr John Kirkhope 1920
NG 1447

Camille COROT
(1796–1875) French
Souvenir of the Environs of La Ferté-sous-Jouarre (Morning)
Oil on canvas: 45.8 x 60.5
Signed
Bequest of Dr John Kirkhope 1920
NG 1448

Camille COROT
(1796–1875) French
The Ruin
Oil on canvas: 40.4 x 54
Signed
Bequest of Dr John Kirkhope 1920
NG 1449

Camille COROT
(1796–1875) French
Gathering Primroses
Oil on panel: 28.3 x 47
Signed
Bequest of Dr John Kirkhope 1920
NG 1450

Camille COROT
(1796–1875) French
Ville-d'Avray: Entrance to the Wood
Oil on canvas: 46 x 35
With signature
Purchased with the aid of A. E. Anderson
in memory of his brother Frank 1927
NG 1681

Camille COROT
(1796–1875) French
The Artist's Mother (Marie Françoise Oberson, 1769–1851)
Oil on canvas: 40.8 x 33
Signed
Purchased 1936
NG 1852

Attributed to Camille COROT
(1796–1875) French
Evening Landscape
Oil on canvas: 45 x 35
With signature
Bequest of Dr John Kirkhope 1920
NG 1451

Attributed to Camille COROT
(1796–1875) French
The Watering Place
Oil on canvas: 24.5 x 32.5
With signature
Bequest of Dr John Kirkhope 1920
NG 1452

Follower of Camille COROT
(1796–1875) French
Landscape with Two Cows
Oil on canvas: 26.1 x 39.4
With signature
Bequest of Hugh A. Laird 1911
NG 1039

Attributed to CORREGGIO (Antonio Allegri)
(*c.* 1489–1534) Italian
An Allegory of Virtue
Oil on panel: 100 x 83 (unfinished)
Purchased 1993
NG 2584

John Sell COTMAN
(1782–1842) English
Buildings on a River
Oil on canvas: 36.2 x 31.1
Presented by the National Art Collections
Fund 1905
NG 931

John Sell COTMAN
(1782–1842) English
The Meadow
Oil on canvas: 32.7 x 47
Purchased 1913
NG 1135

Circle of John Sell COTMAN
(1782–1842) English
Lakenham Mills
Oil on canvas: 34.3 x 45.5
Purchased 1908
NG 960

Gustave COURBET
(1819–77) French
A River in a Gorge
Oil on canvas: 81.4 x 64.7
Signed
Presented by Sir Alexander Maitland in memory
of his wife Rosalind 1960
NG 2232

Gustave COURBET
(1819–77) French
The Wave
Oil on canvas: 46 x 55
Signed
Presented by Sir Alexander Maitland in memory
of his wife Rosalind 1960
NG 2233

Gustave COURBET
(1819–77) French
Trees in the Snow
Oil on canvas: 72.3 x 91.5
Signed
Presented by Sir Alexander Maitland in memory
of his wife Rosalind 1960
NG 2234

Jacques COURTOIS (Il Borgognone)
(1621–76) French
A Battle
Oil on canvas: 94 x 149
Bequest of Mrs Mary Veitch to the RSA 1875;
transferred and presented 1910
NG 621

Thomas COUTURE
(1815–79) French
Portrait of a Lady ('Une Patricienne')
Oil on canvas: 63.8 x 55
Signed with initials and dated 1852
Bequest of William Leiper 1916
NG 1202

Lucas CRANACH the Elder
(1472–1553) German
Venus and Cupid
Oil on panel: 38.1 x 27
Signed with a cipher
Bequest of the 11th Marquess of Lothian 1941
NG 1942

Edmund Thornton CRAWFORD
(1806–85) Scottish
A Group of Trees at Grange
Oil on panel: 27.3 x 40
Purchased by the RI 1826; transferred 1859
NG 176

Edmund Thornton CRAWFORD
(1806–85) Scottish
Closehauled: Crossing the Bar
Oil on canvas: 61 x 92.1
Purchased by RAPFAS 1861; transferred 1897
NG 421

Gaspar de CRAYER
(1584–1669) Flemish
The Assumption of St Catherine
Oil on canvas: 75 x 47.3
Presented by Alexander Wood Inglis 1918
NG 1211

John CROME
(1768–1821) English
A Mountain Scene
Oil on canvas: 75.3 x 59.1
Purchased 1907
NG 944

John CROME
(1768–1821) English
The Beaters
Oil on panel: 54.6 x 86.4
Purchased 1970
NG 2309

John CROME
(1768–1821) English
A Sandy Bank
Oil on canvas: 36.7 x 52.4
Purchased 1988
NG 2459

Sir Stanley CURSITER
(1887–1976) Scottish
Twilight
Oil on canvas: 152.3 x 214
Signed and dated 1914
Purchased 1987
NG 2452

Sir Stanley CURSITER
(1887–1976) Scottish
*The Interior of the National Gallery
of Scotland, c. 1937*
Reverse: *The Interior of the National Gallery
of Scotland* (see next item)
Oil on plyboard: 40.5 x 30.5
Purchased by the Patrons of the National Galleries
of Scotland 1988
NG 2466

Sir Stanley CURSITER
(1887–1976) Scottish
*The Interior of the National Gallery
of Scotland*
Reverse of NG 2466

Aelbert CUYP
(1620–91) Dutch
Landscape with a View of the Valkhof, Nijmegen
Oil on canvas: 113 x 165
Signed
Purchased with the aid of the National Art
Collections Fund 1972 (in recognition of
the services of the Earl of Crawford and Balcarres
to the National Art Collections Fund
and the National Galleries of Scotland)
NG 2314

Bernardo DADDI
(active *c.* 1327 – died 1348) Italian
Triptych. Centre: *The Crucifixion.* Left Wing:
*The Nativity; Two Prophets; The Crucifixion
of St Peter.* Right Wing: *The Virgin and Child
Enthroned with Saints; Two Prophets; St Nicholas
Donating the Dowries.* Pinnacle: *Christ Blessing*
Tempera, silver and gold on panel:
53.5 x 28 (centre); 58 x 15.5 (left wing);
57.5 x 15.2 (right wing)
Inscribed and dated 1338
Purchased 1938
NG 1904

Charles-François DAUBIGNY
(1817–78) French
A View of Herblay
Oil on panel: 38.8 x 67.2
Signed and dated 1869
Bequest of Hugh A. Laird 1911
NG 1035

Charles-François DAUBIGNY
(1817–78) French
Sunset
Oil on panel: 24.5 x 46.1
Signed and dated 1874
Bequest of Hugh A. Laird 1911
NG 1036

Charles-François DAUBIGNY
(1817–78) French
Cottages at Barbizon: Evening
Oil on panel: 25 x 41.5
Signed
Purchased 1912
NG 1076

Charles-François DAUBIGNY
(1817–78) French
A Village by a River at Sunset
Oil on panel: 24 x 49.9
Signed
Bequest of Dr John Kirkhope 1920
NG 1453

Charles-François DAUBIGNY
(1817–78) French
Orchard in Blossom
Oil on canvas: 85 x 157
Signed and dated 1874
Purchased 1993
NG 2586

Honoré DAUMIER
(1808–79) French
The Painter
Oil on panel: 28.9 x 18.7
Presented by the National Art Collections
Fund 1923
NG 1616

Honoré DAUMIER
(1808–79) French
The Serenade
Oil on panel: 30.5 x 39.8
Transferred from the Tate Gallery 1988
NG 2453

Gerard DAVID
(*c.* 1460–1523) Netherlandish
Three Legends of St Nicholas: He gives thanks to
God on the day of his birth; He slips a purse
through the window of an impoverished nobleman
as dowry for his daughters; As Bishop
of Myra, he resuscitates three boys salted down
as meat in a famine
Oil on panel: 55.9 x 33.7 (each panel)
Purchased with the aid of the National Art
Collections Fund and a Treasury Grant 1959
NG 2213

Alexandre-Gabriel DECAMPS
(1803–60) French
The Beggars
Oil on panel: 17 x 27.4
Signed and dated 1849
Bequest of Hugh A. Laird 1911
NG 1045

Edgar DEGAS
(1834–1917) French
Diego Martelli (1839–96)
Oil on canvas: 110.4 x 99.8
With studio stamp
Purchased 1932
NG 1785

Edgar DEGAS
(1834–1917) French
Before the Performance
Oil on paper laid on canvas: 47.6 x 62.5
With studio stamp
Presented by Sir Alexander Maitland in memory
of his wife Rosalind 1960
NG 2224

Edgar DEGAS
(1834–1917) French
A Group of Dancers
Oil on paper laid on canvas: 47 x 61.90 cm
With studio stamp
Presented by Sir Alexander Maitland in memory
of his wife Rosalind 1960
NG 2225

Edgar DEGAS
(1834–1917) French
A Study of a Girl's Head
Oil on canvas: 57.1 x 45
With studio stamp
Presented by Sir Alexander Maitland in memory
of his wife Rosalind 1960
NG 2227

Eugène DELACROIX
(1798–1863) French
Arabs Playing Chess
Oil on canvas: 46 x 55
Signed
Purchased 1957
NG 2190

Eugène DELACROIX
(1798–1863) French
A Vase of Flowers
Oil on canvas: 57.7 x 48.8
Signed and dated 1833
Purchased 1980
NG 2405

Dirck van DELEN
(1605–71) Dutch
A Conversation in a Palace Courtyard
Oil on panel: 54 x 47
Signed and dated 1644
Purchased by the RI 1830; transferred 1859
NG 111

William DENUNE
(c. 1715–50) Scottish
Portrait of a Young Lady
Oil on canvas: 55.9 x 44.5
Signed and dated 1745
Purchased 1942
NG 1966

William DENUNE
(*c.* 1715–50) Scottish
Portrait of a Gentleman
Oil on canvas: 75.6 x 62.2
Signed and dated 1745
Purchased 1945
NG 2037

Marcellin DESBOUTIN
(1823–1902) French
Mother and Child
Oil on canvas: 45.6 x 37.8
Signed
Purchased 1913
NG 1130

Narcisse DIAZ de la Peña
(1807–76) French
A Clearing in the Forest
Oil on panel: 27 x 40.8
Signed and dated 1869
Bequest of Hugh A. Laird 1911
NG 1042

Narcisse DIAZ de la Peña
(1807–76) French
A Pool in the Forest
Oil on panel: 24.3 x 32.5
Signed
Bequest of Hugh A. Laird 1911
NG 1043

Narcisse DIAZ de la Peña
(1807–76) French
Turkish Children
Oil on canvas: 22.5 x 17.5
Signed
Bequest of Hugh A. Laird 1911
NG 1044

Narcisse DIAZ de la Peña
(1807–76) French
Flowers
Oil on canvas: 47 x 37.8
Signed with initials
Bequest of Dr John Kirkhope 1920
NG 1454

Christian Wilhelm DIETRICH (Dietricy)
(1712–74) German
St Boniface Felling the Sacred Oak
Oil on canvas: 74.4 x 104.5
Bequest of Mrs Mary Veitch to the RSA 1875;
transferred and presented 1910
NG 619

DOMENICHINO (Domenico Zampieri)
(1581–1641) Italian
The Adoration of the Shepherds
Oil on canvas: 143 x 115
Purchased 1971
NG 2313

John Milne DONALD
(1819–66) Scottish
A Highland Stream: Glenfruin
Oil on canvas: 64.8 x 89.9
Signed and dated 1861
Purchased 1909
NG 987

Gerrit DOU
(1613–75) Dutch
An Interior with a Young Violinist
Oil on panel: 31.1 x 23.7 (arched)
Signed and dated 1637
Purchased with the aid of the National Heritage
Memorial Fund 1984
NG 2420

Thomas DOUGHTY
(1793–1856) American
A View of the Flat Rock on the Schuylkill,
near Philadelphia
Oil on canvas: 71.2 x 101.8
Signed and dated 1827
Presented to the RI by Philip Teddyman 1828;
transferred 1859
NG 179

Sir William Fettes DOUGLAS
(1822–91) Scottish
The Spell
Oil on canvas: 77.5 x 157
Signed in monogram with cipher and dated 1864
Presented by James T. Gibson-Craig 1886
NG 779

Sir William Fettes DOUGLAS
(1822–91) Scottish
Stonehaven Harbour
Oil on canvas: 119.4 x 58.8
Purchased 1909
NG 981

Sir William Fettes DOUGLAS
(1822–91) Scottish
A Street in Rome
Oil on panel: 16.5 x 10.2
Inscribed, signed in monogram and dated 1857
Transferred and presented by the RSA 1910
NG 1002

Sir William Fettes DOUGLAS
(1822–91) Scottish
Wishart Preaching against Mariolatry
Oil on canvas: 78.1 x 175
Reverse: inscribed and dated 1871
Presented by Dr John Kirkhope 1910
NG 1020

Sir William Fettes DOUGLAS
(1822–91) Scottish
*Hudibras and Ralph Visiting the Astrologer
(from Butler's 'Hudibras')*
Oil on canvas: 64.8 x 105.5
Signed in monogram with cipher and dated 1856
Bequest of Dr John Kirkhope 1920
NG 1479

Sir William Fettes DOUGLAS
(1822–91) Scottish
Bric-a-brac
Oil on canvas: 20.5 x 41.4
Signed in monogram with cipher and dated 1862
Reverse: inscribed
Bequest of Alexander F. Roberts 1929
NG 1731

Sir William Fettes DOUGLAS
(1822–91) Scottish
The Head of a Woman
Oil on canvas: 14 x 14
Bequest of Mrs M. B. Stuart 1938
NG 1896

James DRUMMOND
(1816–77) Scottish
The Porteous Mob
Oil on canvas: 111.8 x 152.5
Signed and dated 1855
Purchased by RAPFAS 1856; transferred 1897
NG 180

James DRUMMOND
(1816–77) Scottish
*James Graham, 1st Marquis of Montrose
(1612–50)*
Oil on canvas: 113 x 186
Signed and dated 1859
Bequest of the artist 1877
NG 624

James DRUMMOND
(1816–77) Scottish
The Return of Mary Queen of Scots to Edinburgh
Oil on canvas: 86.4 x 125.1
Signed and dated 1870
Bequest of the artist 1877
NG 625

Gaspard DUGHET (Gaspard Poussin)
(1615–75) French
Classical Landscape with a Lake
Oil on canvas: 73 x 99.5
Purchased 1973
NG 2318

Circle of Gaspard DUGHET (Gaspard Poussin)
(1615–75) French
Landscape with the Triumph of Bacchus
Oil on canvas: 96.2 x 134
Purchased by the RI 1830; transferred 1859
NG 62

Follower of Gaspard DUGHET (Gaspard Poussin)
(1615–75) French
River Landscape with a Hunt
Oil on canvas: 109.8 x 133.7
Presented to the RSA by Robert Clouston 1850;
transferred and presented 1910
NG 38

Follower of Gaspard DUGHET (Gaspard Poussin)
(1615–75) French
Classical Landscape
Oil on canvas: 120.3 x 171
Bequest of Mrs Nisbet Hamilton Ogilvy
of Biel 1921
NG 1512

Henry G. DUGUID
(active 1828–60) Scottish
Old Trinity Church, Edinburgh
Oil on millboard: 21.6 x 29.2
Signed and dated 1848
Purchased 1936
NG 1839

John DUNCAN
(1866–1945) Scottish
Angus Og, God of Love and Courtesy,
Putting a Spell of Summer Calm on the Sea
Oil on canvas: 152.4 x 101.6
Signed and dated 1908
Bequest of the artist 1946
NG 2033

John DUNCAN
(1866–1945) Scottish
St Bride
Tempera on canvas: 122.3 x 144.5
Signed and dated 1913
Purchased 1946
NG 2043

Thomas DUNCAN
(1807–45) Scottish
The Entombment of Christ (after Titian)
Oil on canvas: 80.3 x 115.9
Reverse: signed with initials
Purchased by the Board of Manufactures
for the Trustees' Academy 1846;
transferred 1859
NG 106

Thomas DUNCAN
(1807–45) Scottish
'Allegory of the Marqués del Vasto' (after Titian)
Oil on canvas: 61 x 50.8
Purchased by the Board of Manufactures
for the Trustees' Academy 1846;
transferred 1859
NG 107

Thomas DUNCAN
(1807–45) Scottish
The Marriage at Cana (after Veronese)
Oil on canvas: 86.6 x 121.9
Reverse: signed with initials
Probably acquired by the RI c. 1845;
transferred 1859
NG 128

Thomas DUNCAN
(1807–45) Scottish
Self-portrait
Oil on canvas: 128.7 x 102
Signed and dated 1844
Purchased and presented by fifty Scottish artists
to the RSA 1845; transferred and presented 1910
NG 182

Thomas DUNCAN
(1807–45) Scottish
Anne Page Inviting Slender to Dinner
Oil on panel: 134.3 x 103.5
Signed and dated 1836
Purchased by the RSA 1861;
transferred and presented 1910
NG 448

Thomas DUNCAN
(1807–45) Scottish
Katherine Munro, Lady Steuart of Allanbank
Oil on canvas: 74.7 x 61
Presented to the RSA by James T. Gibson-Craig
1863; transferred and presented 1910
NG 466

Thomas DUNCAN
(1807–45) Scottish
Braan, a Celebrated Scottish Deerhound
Oil on canvas: 127.3 x 167.6
Bequest of Duncan MacNeill, Lord Colonsay 1874
NG 604

Thomas DUNCAN
(1807–45) Scottish
Self-portrait (after Rembrandt)
Oil on canvas: 32.4 x 28
Bequest of Mary Hamilton Campbell,
Baroness Ruthven 1885
NG 707

Jules DUPRÉ
(1811–89) French
A Fisherman
Oil on canvas: 46.3 x 38.3
Signed
Bequest of Hugh A. Laird 1911
NG 1040

Jules DUPRÉ
(1811–89) French
The Windmill
Oil on panel: 22.2 x 35
Signed
Bequest of Hugh A. Laird 1911
NG 1041

DUTCH School
(17th century)
Still Life
Oil on canvas: 62.3 x 53.4
Purchased 1909
NG 989

DUTCH School
(17th century)
The Toast
Oil on panel: 36.9 x 29.3
Bequest of Mrs Nisbet Hamilton Ogilvy
of Biel 1921
NG 1510

DUTCH School
(17th century)
Two Peasants Smoking by a Fire
('Silent Companions')
Oil on canvas laid on panel: 16.5 x 14.6
Presented by the National Art Collections
Fund 1928
NG 1686

DUTCH School
(17th century)
Portrait of a Man
Oil on panel: 40.1 x 33.3
Purchased 1935
NG 1832

DUTCH School
(17th century)
Still Life
Oil on panel: 40.5 x 32.6
Bequest of the 11th Marquess of Lothian 1941
NG 1932

DUTCH School
(17th century)
An Old Lady Wearing a Ruff
Oil on panel: 51.3 x 44.4
Lent by the Duke of Sutherland 1945

William DYCE
(1806–64) Scottish
The Infant Hercules
Oil on canvas: 92 x 71.8
Presented by Sir John Hay, 6th Bart of Smithfield
and Hayston to the RI 1831; transferred 1859
NG 184

William DYCE
(1806–64) Scottish
Francesca da Rimini
Oil on canvas: 142 x 176
Purchased by the RSA 1864;
transferred and presented 1910
NG 460

William DYCE
(1806–64) Scottish
The Judgement of Solomon
Tempera on paper laid on canvas: 151.2 x 245
Presented by Professor Goodsir to the RSA 1864;
transferred and presented 1910
NG 521

William DYCE
(1806–64) Scottish
Shirrapburn Loch
Oil on millboard: 30.5 x 40.6
Presented by Charles Guthrie 1961
NG 2199

William DYCE
(1806–64) Scottish
St Catherine
Oil on panel: 88.9 x 64.8
Purchased 1964
NG 2267

William DYCE
(1806–64) Scottish
*Two Heads from 'The Consecration of Archbishop
Parker in Lambeth Chapel AD 1559'*
Fresco secco on lath and plaster: 73.7 x 91.5
Purchased 1979
NG 2395

William DYCE
(1806–64) Scottish
David in the Wilderness (companion-piece
to NG 2410)
Oil on millboard: 34.3 x 49.5
Purchased with the aid of the National Heritage
Purchase Grant (Scotland) 1981
NG 2409

William DYCE
(1806–64) Scottish
Man of Sorrows (companion-piece to NG 2409)
Oil on millboard: 34.3 x 49.5
Purchased with the aid of the National Heritage
Purchase Grant (Scotland) 1981
NG 2410

William DYCE
(1806–64) Scottish
King Lear and the Fool in the Storm
Oil on canvas: 136 x 173
Purchased with the aid of the National Art
Collections Fund 1993
NG 2585

Sir Anthony van DYCK
(1599–1641) Flemish
An Italian Noble
Oil on canvas: 237.6 x 154.3
Purchased by the RI 1830; transferred 1859
NG 119

Sir Anthony van DYCK
(1599–1641) Flemish
'The Lomellini Family'
Oil on canvas: 269 x 254
Purchased by the RI 1830; transferred 1859
NG 120

Sir Anthony van DYCK
(1599–1641) Flemish
St Sebastian Bound for Martyrdom
Oil on canvas: 226 x 160
Purchased by the RI 1830; transferred 1859
NG 121

Attributed to Sir Anthony van DYCK
(1599–1641) Flemish
A Study of a Head
Oil on canvas: 42.5 x 37.5
Purchased by the RI 1846; transferred 1859
NG 122

Attributed to Sir Anthony van DYCK
(1599–1641) Flemish
Portrait of a Young Man
Oil on canvas laid on panel: 77.5 x 56
Lent by the Duke of Sutherland 1945

Studio of Sir Anthony van DYCK
(1599–1641) Flemish
Marchese Ambrogio Spinola (1569–1630)
Oil on canvas: 121.9 x 96.5
Purchased by the RI 1830; transferred 1859
NG 87

After Sir Anthony van DYCK
(1599–1641) Flemish
*Geneviève d'Urfé, Duchesse de Croy
(died before 1656)*
Oil on canvas: 113 x 90.2
With inscription
Bequest of the 11th Marquess of Lothian 1941
NG 1944

Adam ELSHEIMER
(1578–1610) German
The Stoning of St Stephen
Oil on tinned copper: 34.7 x 28.6
Purchased 1965
NG 2281

Adam ELSHEIMER
(1578–1610) German
Il Contento
Oil on copper: 30 x 42
Accepted in lieu of tax 1970
NG 2312

Imitator of Adam ELSHEIMER
(1578–1610) German
The Young Virgin Mary with St Anne
Oil on copper: 10.3 x 7.7
Transferred from the SNPG 1996
NG 2653

EMILIAN School
(15th century)
*The Virgin and Child with St Francis,
St Jerome and Two Angels*
Panel: 115.5 x 92.8
Bequest of Sir Claude Phillips 1924
NG 1634

EMILIAN School
(17th century)
The Deliverance of St Peter
Oil on canvas: 108 x 94.5
Purchased by the RI 1840; transferred 1859
NG 19

John EMMS
(1843–1912) English
Callum
Oil on canvas: 69.9 x 90.2
Inscribed, signed and dated 1895
Bequest of James Cowan Smith 1919
NG 1226

William ETTY
(1787–1849) English
St John the Baptist Preaching (after Veronese)
Oil on canvas. 69.2 x 54
Purchased by the RSA 1853;
transferred and presented 1910
NG 127

William ETTY
(1787–1849) English
Judith's Maid outside the Tent of Holofernes
Oil on canvas: 300 x 274
Commissioned by the RSA 1830;
transferred and presented 1910
NG 185

William ETTY
(1787–1849) English
Judith and Holofernes
Oil on canvas: 299 x 392
Purchased by the RSA 1829;
transferred and presented 1910
NG 186

William ETTY
(1787–1849) English
Judith Coming Out of the Tent
Oil on canvas: 300 x 274
Commissioned by the RSA 1830;
transferred and presented 1910
NG 187

William ETTY
(1787–1849) English
Benaiah Slaying Two Lion-like Men of Moab
Oil on canvas: 255 x 341
Purchased by the RSA 1831;
transferred and presented 1910
NG 188

William ETTY
(1787–1849) English
*The Combat: Woman Pleading for
the Vanquished*
Oil on canvas: 304 x 399
Purchased by the RSA 1831;
transferred and presented 1910
NG 189

John Wilson EWBANK
(1799–1847) Scottish
A Harbour Scene with Shipping
Oil on millboard laid on panel: 30 x 45.2
Presented by John Inglis, Lord Glencorse 1883
NG 672

John Wilson EWBANK
(1799–1847) Scottish
On the East Coast
Oil on panel: 25.2 x 35.7
Transferred and presented by the RSA 1910
NG 1007

François-Xavier FABRE
(1766–1837) French
Portrait of a Man
Oil on canvas: 61.5 x 50
Signed and dated 1809
Purchased with the aid of the National Art
Collections Fund 1992
NG 2548

James FAED
(1821–1911) Scottish
The Artist's Son (William Cotton Faed,
1858–1937)
Oil on millboard: 31.1 x 25.1
Signed and dated 1870
Presented by Mr and Mrs Ian Faed 1985
NG 2425

John FAED
(1819–1902) Scottish
The Evening Hour (Portrait Group of the Children
of Dr Archibald Bennie)
Watercolour and gum on ivory set into panel:
33 x 24.2
Presented by J. Bray 1914
NG 1142

John FAED
(1819–1902) Scottish
Queen Margaret's Defiance of the Scottish
Parliament
Oil on canvas: 75.6 x 99.3
Purchased 1991
NG 2527

John FAED
(1819–1902) Scottish
A Study for 'Queen Margaret's Defiance of the Scottish Parliament' (NG 2527)
Oil on millboard laid on panel: 28 x 34.3
Signed
Purchased 1995
NG 2634

Thomas FAED (1826–1900) and John MACDONALD (born 1821)
Scottish
Four Saints (St George, St Catherine, St Margaret and St Andrew), after designs by Alexander Christie and S. Rice
Oil on canvas: 208 x 38.1; 216 x 38.1; 216 x 38.1; 208 x 38.1
Presented by Alexander Christie 1859
NG 175

Thomas FAED
(1826–1900) Scottish
Home and the Homeless
Oil on canvas: 66.7 x 95.6
Signed and dated 1856
Purchased 1992
NG 2549

Thomas FAED
(1826–1900) Scottish
A Life Study of John Mongo ('The Punka-walla')
Oil on paper laid on board: 66 x 52.8
With inscription and date 1847
Purchased 1993
NG 2560

Henri FANTIN-LATOUR
(1836–1904) French
Roses
Oil on canvas: 38 x 40
Signed
Bequest of Dr John Kirkhope 1920
NG 1455

Henri FANTIN-LATOUR
(1836–1904) French
Spring Flowers
Oil on canvas: 25.5 x 25
Signed and dated 1872
Bequest of Dr John Kirkhope 1920
NG 1456

Henri FANTIN-LATOUR
(1836–1904) French
Peaches on a Dish
Oil on panel: 23.9 x 33.2
Signed and dated 1873
Bequest of the Revd H. G. R. Hay-Boyd 1941
NG 1950

Henri FANTIN-LATOUR
(1836–1904) French
Roses
Oil on canvas: 46.4 x 40.5
Signed and dated 1888
Presented by Miss Elizabeth Sutherland 1948
NG 2107

David FARQUHARSON
(1840–1907) Scottish
A Cornish Valley
Oil on canvas: 44.5 x 75
Signed and dated 1902
Bequest of Hugh A. Laird 1911
NG 1063

William Gouw FERGUSON
(*c.* 1632/33– after 1695) Scottish
A Ruined Altar and Figures
Oil on canvas: 68.6 x 53.7
Presented by Alexander White to the RSA 1858;
transferred and presented 1910
NG 190

William Gouw FERGUSON
(*c.* 1632/33– after 1695) Scottish
Still Life: Dead Game
Oil on canvas: 66 x 53.4
Signed and dated 1684
Purchased 1908
NG 970

William Gouw FERGUSON
(*c.* 1632/33– after 1635) Scottish
Still Life: Dead Game
Oil on canvas: 105.4 x 85.8
Signed
Presented by Arthur Kay 1910
NG 1029

William Gouw FERGUSON
(*c.* 1632/33– after 1635) Scottish
Still Life: Dead Game
Oil on canvas: 149.9 x 121.9
Signed and dated 1677
Presented by Frederick John Nettlefold 1947
NG 2096

FERRARESE School
(15th century)
The Virgin and Child with Two Angels
Panel: 58.5 x 44
Purchased 1921
NG 1535

Anthony Vandyke Copley FIELDING
(1787–1855) English
Newark Castle
Oil on panel: 17.2 x 22.3
Signed
Purchased 1932
NG 1786

FLEMISH School
(17th century)
The Raising of the Cross
Oil on canvas: 46.5 x 36
Presented to the RI by James Johnston before 1845;
transferred 1859
NG 108

FLEMISH School
(17th century)
A Cavalier in a Yellow Coat
Oil on canvas: 69.3 x 56
Bequest of Alexander Wood Inglis 1929
NG 1728

Gerlach FLICKE
(died 1558) German
Lord Grey de Wilton (c. 1508–62)
Oil on panel: 104.5 x 79.6
Inscribed, signed and dated 1547
Bequest of the 11th Marquess of Lothian 1941
NG 1933

Gerlach FLICKE
(died 1558) German
Sir Peter Carew (1514–75)
Oil on panel: 86 x 58.2
Bequest of the 11th Marquess of Lothian 1941
NG 1934

FLORENTINE School
(16th century)
The Virgin and Child with the Infant St John the Baptist
Oil on panel: 87.5 (circular)
Bequest of David Laing 1879
NG 645

Jean-Louis FORAIN
(1852–1931) French
A Lady in a Fur Cape
Oil on canvas: 22 x 16.4
Inscribed and signed
Bequest of R. H. Walpole 1963
NG 2266

Anne FORBES
(1745–1834) Scottish
Lady Anne Stewart (1703–83)
Oil on canvas: 75 x 62.3
Purchased 1945
NG 2036

Mariano FORTUNY
(1838–74) Spanish
Le Brindis de L'Espada (The Bull-fighter's Salute)
Oil on canvas: 100 x 67
With signature and studio stamp
Purchased 1915
NG 1189

Alexander FRASER the Elder
(1786–1865) Scottish
Portrait of a Young Man
Oil on panel: 16.3 x 12.5
Reverse: signed and dated 1816
Presented by J. C. Wardrop 1937
NG 1887

Alexander FRASER the Elder
(1786–1865) Scottish
Portrait of a Young Man
Oil on panel: 16.5 x 12.7
Presented by J. C. Wardrop 1937
NG 1888

Alexander FRASER the Elder
(1786–1865) Scottish
A Highland Sportsman
Oil on panel: 78.1 x 109.3
Signed and dated 1832
Purchased 1951
NG 2134

Alexander FRASER the Younger
(1827–99) Scottish
An Entrance to Cadzow Forest
Oil on canvas: 64.8 x 90.2
Signed
Purchased 1915
NG 1188

Alexander FRASER the Younger
(1827–99) Scottish
A Glade in Cadzow Forest
Oil on canvas: 69.9 x 92.1
Signed
Reverse: with inscription
Bequest of Dr John Kirkhope 1920
NG 1480

Alexander FRASER the Younger
(1827–99) Scottish
A Sheepfold, Haslemere
Oil on canvas: 24.8 x 35
Signed
Bequest of Dr John Kirkhope 1920
NG 1481

Alexander FRASER the Younger
(1827–99) Scottish
Haymaking on the Avon
Oil on canvas: 89.8 x 119.4 (painted area)
Signed
Purchased 1942
NG 1980

Alexander FRASER the Younger
(1827–99) Scottish
Atholl
Oil on canvas: 22.5 x 33
Signed with initials
Reverse: signed
Bequest of Dr Robert A. Lillie 1977
NG 2352

FRENCH School
(17th century)
The Death of King Laius
Oil on canvas: 59.7 x 59.7
Purchased 1935
NG 1829

FRENCH School
(16th century)
George, 5th Lord Seton (c. 1531–85), aged 27
Oil on panel: 120 x 105.7
Inscribed and dated 157[ ]
Bequest of Sir Theophilus Biddulph 1948;
received 1965
NG 2274

FRENCH School
(19th century)
The Entombment of Christ
Oil on canvas: 32.4 x 39.7
Purchased with the aid of the Cowan Smith
Bequest Fund 1927
NG 1667

Francesco FURINI
(1603–46) Italian
St Sebastian
Oil on canvas: 50.5 x 38.5
Purchased by the RI 1831; transferred 1859
NG 30

Francesco FURINI
(1603–46) Italian
Poetry
Oil on paper laid on panel: 41.4 x 34.5
Purchased by the RI 1831; transferred 1859
NG 31

Jan FYT
(1611–61) Flemish
A Wolf
Oil on canvas: 92.7 x 74.3 (fragment)
Purchased by the RSA 1866;
transferred and presented 1910
NG 529

Jan FYT
(1611–61) Flemish
A Dead Wolf
Oil on canvas: 60.4 x 92.1 (fragment)
Purchased by the RSA 1866;
transferred and presented 1910
NG 530

Thomas GAINSBOROUGH
(1727–88) English
The Hon. Mrs Graham (1757–92)
Oil on canvas: 237 x 154
Bequest of Robert Graham of Redgorton 1859
NG 332

Thomas GAINSBOROUGH
(1727–88) English
Mrs Hamilton Nisbet (1756–1834)
Oil on canvas: 233 x 155
Bequest of Mrs Nisbet Hamilton Ogilvy
of Biel 1921
NG 1521

Thomas GAINSBOROUGH
(1727–88) English
Landscape with a View of a Distant Village
Oil on canvas: 75 x 151
Purchased 1953
NG 2174

Thomas GAINSBOROUGH
(1727–88) English
Rocky Landscape
Oil on canvas: 119.4 x 147.3
Purchased with the aid of a Treasury Grant 1962
NG 2253

GAROFALO (Benvenuto Tisi)
(*c.* 1476–1559) Italian
Christ Driving the Moneychangers
from the Temple
Oil on panel: 45.7 x 37.2
Purchased by the RI 1830; transferred 1859
NG 32

Louis GAUFFIER
(1761–1801) French
Cleopatra and Octavian
Oil on canvas: 83.8 x 112.5
Purchased with the aid of the National Art
Collections Fund 1991
NG 2526

Paul GAUGUIN
(1848–1903) French
The Vision after the Sermon (Jacob and the Angel)
Oil on canvas: 72.20 x 91
Signed and dated 1888
Purchased 1925
NG 1643

Paul GAUGUIN
(1848–1903) French
Martinique Landscape
Oil on canvas: 115 x 88.5
Signed and dated 1887
Presented by Sir Alexander Maitland in memory
of his wife Rosalind 1960
NG 2220

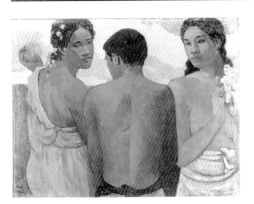

Paul GAUGUIN
(1848–1903) French
Three Tahitians
Oil on canvas: 73 x 94
Signed and dated 1899
Presented by Sir Alexander Maitland in memory
of his wife Rosalind 1960
NG 2221

Andrew GEDDES
(1783–1844) Scottish
Summer
Oil on canvas: 81.3 x 64.2
Purchased by the RI 1828, transferred 1859
NG 191

Andrew GEDDES
(1783–1844) Scottish
George Sanders (1774–1846)
Oil on panel: 70 x 49.5
Signed and dated 1816
Presented by Thomas Menzies to the RSA 1861;
transferred and presented 1910
NG 416

Andrew GEDDES
(1783–1844) Scottish
*The Artist's Mother (Agnes Boyd, Mrs David
Geddes, died 1828)*
Oil on canvas: 72 x 61
Presented by Adela Geddes 1877
NG 630

Andrew GEDDES
(1783–1844) Scottish
Hagar
Oil on canvas: 75.5 x 62.7
Presented by Adela Geddes 1877
NG 631

Andrew GEDDES
(1783–1844) Scottish
Andrew Plimer (1763–1837)
Oil on panel: 47.5 x 39.4
Signed and dated 1815
Purchased 1900
NG 847

Andrew GEDDES
(1783–1844) Scottish
Mrs Douglas Dickson
Oil on canvas: 88.7 x 69.3
Bequest of Sir Andrew Douglas Maclagan 1900
NG 848

Andrew GEDDES
(1783–1844) Scottish
Hannah Fry, Mrs Harris Prendergast (1814–59)
Oil on canvas: 126.5 x 101
Signed with initials and dated 1838
Bequest of Canon Charles Edward Middleton
Fry 1950
NG 2127

Andrew GEDDES
(1783–1844) Scottish
The Artist's Sister (Anne Geddes, 1785–1843)
Oil on canvas: 12 / x 94.7
Presented by Mrs H. F. Rose 1951
NG 2156

Andrew GEDDES
(1783–1844) Scottish
Archibald Scot Skirving (1749–1819)
Oil on canvas: 72.7 x 60
Bequest of A. A. Scot Skirving 1967
NG 2293

Andrew GEDDES
(1783–1844) Scottish
Landscape
Oil on paper laid on panel: 20 x 29.6
Presented by Charles Ballantyne 1973
NG 2320

Andrew GEDDES
(1783–1844) Scottish
Portrait of Two Women
Oil on panel: 20 x 17
Purchased through the Patrons of the National
Galleries of Scotland with the aid of the Scottish
Postal Board 1986
NG 2438

Attributed to Andrew GEDDES
(1783–1844) Scottish
Portrait of a Man
Oil on canvas: 62.2 x 50.8
Bequest of Dr John MacGregor 1942
NG 1967

Follower of GEERTGEN tot Sint Jans
(*c.* 1455/65– *c.* 1485/95) Netherlandish
*The Crucifixion with St Jerome and St Dominic
and Scenes from the Passion*
Oil on panel: 24.4 x 18.4
Purchased 1920
NG 1253

Walter GEIKIE
(1795–1837) Scottish
A Scottish Roadside Scene
Oil on canvas: 40.6 x 61
Signed
Presented by Harold S. Geikie 1935
NG 1825

Walter GEIKIE
(1795–1837) Scottish
The Fruit Seller
Oil on panel: 40.6 x 34.3
Signed and dated 1824
Purchased 1975
NG 2335

François, Baron GÉRARD
(1770–1837) French
Mary Nisbet, Countess of Elgin (1777–1855)
Oil on canvas: 64.8 x 54.6
Bequest of Mrs Nisbet Hamilton Ogilvy
of Biel 1921
NG 1496

François, Baron GÉRARD
(1770–1837) French
Madame Mère (Maria Laetitia Ramolino
Bonaparte, 1750–1836)
Oil on canvas: 210.8 x 129.8
Signed
Purchased with the aid of the National Art
Collections Fund 1988
NG 2461

GERMAN School
(15th century)
Twenty Scenes from the Life of Christ
Oil on panel: 126 x 106.5 (on 5 separate panels)
Presented by the National Museums
of Scotland 1936
NG 2310

GERMAN School
(16th century)
St John with a Donor and his Sons
(companion wing to NG 999)
Oil on panel: 58.5 x 25.7
Purchased 1910
NG 998

GERMAN School
(16th century)
St Andrew with the Donor's Wife and Daughters
(companion wing to NG 998)
Oil on panel: 58.2 x 26.3
Purchased 1910
NG 999

GERMAN School
(16th century)
St Christopher and a Donor
(companion wing to NG 1928 B)
Oil on panel: 53.8 x 22.2
Bequest of the 11th Marquess of Lothian 1941
NG 1928 A

GERMAN School
(16th century)
St Catherine and the Donor's Wife
(companion wing to NG 1928 A)
Oil on panel: 53.8 x 22.2
Bequest of the 11th Marquess of Lothian 1941
NG 1928 B

Robert GIBB
(1801–37) Scottish
Craigmillar Castle from Dalkeith Road
Oil on board: 27.3 x 40
Signed
Purchased by the RI 1826; transferred 1859
NG 193

Robert GIBB
(1845–1932) Scottish
Portrait of a Girl
Oil on canvas: 41.3 x 31.5 (unfinished)
Presented by Sir James Lewis Caw 1939
NG 2194

Robert GIBB
(1845–1932) Scottish
Five Monks
Oil on canvas: 27.2 x 25.8 (unfinished)
Presented by Sir James Lewis Caw 1939
NG 2195

Imitator of GIORGIONE
(active 1507 – died 1510) Italian
A Man Holding a Recorder
Oil on canvas: 45.8 x 34.9
With inscription
Purchased by the RI 1830; transferred 1859
NG 35

André GIROUX
(1801–79) French
Apollo and Daphne
Oil on canvas: 38 x 46
Purchased 1996
NG 2652

GIULIO Romano (Giulio Pippi)
(c. 1499–1546) Italian
*The Holy Family with the Infant St John
the Baptist ('The Novar Madonna')*
Oil and gold on panel: 82.5 x 63.2
Purchased with the aid of the National Heritage
Purchase Grant (Scotland) 1980
NG 2398

Studio of GIULIO Romano (Giulio Pippi)
(*c.* 1499–1546) Italian
Two Heads from the 'Massacre of the Innocents'
Tempera on paper laid on panel: 52.3 x 36.1
Bequest of Sir David Monro to the RSA 1878;
transferred and presented 1910
NG 638

Hugo van der GOES
(active 1467 – died 1482) Netherlandish
The Trinity Altarpiece.
Left wing: *The Holy Trinity of the Broken Body.*
Right wing: *Edward Bonkil with Two Angels.*
See next item for reverses.
Oil on panel: 202 x 100.5 (each panel)
Her Majesty The Queen: lent from the Royal
Collection 1931

Hugo van der GOES
(active 1467 – died 1482) Netherlandish
The Trinity Altarpiece (reverse).
Left wing: *James III, King of Scots (1452–85)
with his son, James (?) presented by St Andrew.*
Right wing: *Margaret of Denmark, Queen of Scots
(1456–86), presented by St George (?).*

Vincent van GOGH
(1853–90) Dutch
Olive Trees
Oil on canvas: 51 x 65.2
Purchased 1934
NG 1803

Vincent van GOGH
(1853–90) Dutch
The Head of a Peasant Woman
Oil on canvas laid on millboard: 46.4 x 35.3
Presented by Sir Alexander Maitland in memory
of his wife Rosalind 1960
NG 2216

Vincent van GOGH
(1853–90) Dutch
Orchard in Blossom (Plum Trees)
Oil on canvas: 54 x 65.2
Presented by Sir Alexander Maitland in memory
of his wife Rosalind 1960
NG 2217

Sir John Watson GORDON
(1788–1864) Scottish
Peter Spalding (died 1826)
Oil on canvas: 75 x 62.2
Commissioned by the RI in 1828; transferred 1859
NG 204

Sir John Watson GORDON
(1788–1864) Scottish
Roderick Gray (1788–1858)
Oil on canvas: 126.3 x 100.3
Bequest of Henry G. Watson 1879
NG 649

Sir John Watson GORDON
(1788–1864) Scottish
Portrait of a Lady
Oil on canvas: 127 x 101
Reverse: with inscription
Bequest of Henry G. Watson 1879
NG 650

Sir John Watson GORDON
(1788–1864) Scottish
Mr Kippen
Oil on canvas: 90.2 x 73.7
Signed and dated 1810
Reverse: inscribed
Purchased 1952
NG 2170

Sir John Watson GORDON
(1788–1864) Scottish
Return from a Foray
Oil on canvas: 100.3 x 126.3
Signed and dated 1827
Purchased 1954
NG 2177

Francisco de GOYA y Lucientes
(1746–1828) Spanish
El médico (The Doctor)
Oil on canvas: 95.8 x 120.2
Purchased 1923
NG 1628

Jan van GOYEN
(1596–1656) Dutch
A River Scene
Oil on panel: 42.6 x 56.5
Signed in monogram and dated 1646
Bequest of Mrs Mary Veitch to the RSA 1875;
transferred and presented 1910
NG 1013

After Jan van GOYEN
(1596–1656) Dutch
A Village with a Church
Oil on panel: 40 x 58.1
Bequest of Mrs Nisbet Hamilton Ogilvy
of Biel 1921
NG 1497

Style of Benozzo GOZZOLI
(1420–97) Italian
Christ on the Road to Calvary
Canvas laid on panel: 72 x 116.1
Purchased 1908
NG 953

Peter GRAHAM
(1836–1921) Scottish
Wandering Shadows
Oil on canvas: 134.6 x 182.9
Signed and dated 1878
Purchased with the aid of the Cowan Smith
Bequest Fund 1944
NG 1986

Peter GRAHAM
(1836–1921) Scottish
O'er Moor and Moss
Oil on canvas: 110.8 x 164.2
Signed and dated 1867
Purchased 1979
NG 2376

Thomas GRAHAM
(1840–1906) Scottish
A Young Bohemian
Oil on canvas: 90.2 x 63.8
Signed and dated 1864
Purchased 1908
NG 957

John GRAHAM GILBERT
(1794–1866) Scottish
John Gibson (1790–1866)
Oil on canvas: 76 x 63.5
Signed and dated 1847
Presented by the artist to the RSA 1852; transferred
and presented 1910
NG 198

El GRECO (Domenikos Theotokopoulos)
(1541–1614) Spanish
St Jerome in Penitence
Oil on canvas: 104.2 x 96.5
Purchased 1936
NG 1873

El GRECO (Domenikos Theotokopoulos)
(1541–1614) Spanish
Christ Blessing ('The Saviour of the World')
Oil on canvas: 73 x 56.5
Signed with Greek initials
Purchased 1952
NG 2160

El GRECO (Domenikos Theotokopoulos)
(1541–1614) Spanish
An Allegory (Fábula)
Oil on canvas: 67.3 x 88.6
Reverse: with inscription
Accepted in lieu of tax with additional funding
from the National Heritage Memorial Fund,
the National Art Collections Fund and Gallery
funds 1989
NG 2491

Jean-Baptiste GREUZE
(1725–1805) French
A Girl with a Dead Canary
Oil on canvas: 53.3 x 46 (oval)
Bequest of Lady Murray of Henderland 1861
NG 435

Jean-Baptiste GREUZE
(1725–1805) French
A Boy with a Lesson-book
Oil on canvas: 62.5 x 49
Bequest of Lady Murray of Henderland 1861
NG 436

Jean-Baptiste GREUZE
(1725–1805) French
A Girl with Joined Hands
Oil on canvas: 46 x 37.5
Bequest of Lady Murray of Henderland 1861
NG 437

After Jean-Baptiste GREUZE
(1725–1805) French
The Broken Pitcher
Oil on canvas: 40 x 32.9
Bequest of Lady Murray of Henderland 1861
NG 438

Attributed to Jacob or Abel GRIMMER
(c. 1525–90 or c. 1575–1619) Flemish
A Flemish Village
Oil on panel: 34.9 x 48.5
Presented by Sir James Lewis Caw 1946
NG 2040

Alexis GRIMOU
(1678–1733) French
Self-portrait as a Drinker ('The Toper')
Oil on canvas: 116.5 x 89.5
Presented by William Wright 1881
NG 664

Francesco GUARDI
(1712–93) Italian
Santa Maria della Salute, Venice
Oil on canvas: 50.5 x 40.9
Bequest of Mrs Nisbet Hamilton Ogilvy
of Biel 1921
NG 1498

Francesco GUARDI
(1712–93) Italian
San Giorgio Maggiore, Venice
Oil on canvas: 49.5 x 40
Bequest of Mrs Nisbet Hamilton Ogilvy
of Biel 1921
NG 1499

Francesco GUARDI
(1712–93) Italian
Piazza San Marco, Venice
Oil on canvas: 55.2 x 85.4
Accepted in lieu of tax 1978
NG 2370

Style of Francesco GUARDI
(1712–93) Italian
An Italian Capriccio
Oil on canvas: 25.2 x 41.2
Purchased 1891
NG 828

Style of Francesco GUARDI
(1712–93) Italian
An Italian Capriccio
Oil on canvas: 25.2 x 41.2
Purchased 1891
NG 829

GUERCINO (Giovanni Francesco Barbieri)
(1591–1666) Italian
St Peter in Penitence
Oil on canvas: 103.7 x 85.8
Purchased by the RI 1831; transferred 1859
NG 39

GUERCINO (Giovanni Francesco Barbieri)
(1591–1666) Italian
*The Virgin and Child with the Infant St John
the Baptist*
Oil on canvas: 86.5 x 110
Purchased by the RI 1830; transferred 1859
NG 40

GUERCINO (Giovanni Francesco Barbieri)
(1591–1666) Italian
Erminia Finding the Wounded Tancred
Oil on canvas: 244 x 287
Purchased by Private Treaty with the aid of the
Heritage Lottery Fund, the National Art
Collections Fund and corporate and private
donations 1996
NG 2656

Paul-Camille GUIGOU
(1834–71) French
The Olive Trees
Oil on canvas: 68.2 x 104.1
Signed and dated 1860
Purchased 1988
NG 2462

Sir James GUTHRIE
(1859–1930) Scottish
*The Artist's Mother (Anne Orr,
Mrs John Guthrie, 1817–96)*
Oil on canvas: 92 x 72
Signed
Purchased 1944
NG 2017

Sir James GUTHRIE
(1859–1930) Scottish
Pastoral
Oil on canvas: 64.7 x 95.3
Signed
Purchased 1944
NG 2018

Sir James GUTHRIE
(1859–1930) Scottish
Oban
Oil on canvas: 57.3 x 45.9
Signed and dated 1893
Purchased 1947
NG 2087

Sir James GUTHRIE
(1859–1930) Scottish
Revd Dr Andrew Gardiner (died 1892)
Oil on canvas: 124.5 x 97.1
Signed and dated 1888
Bequest of Lady Gardiner 1947
NG 2088

Sir James GUTHRIE
(1859–1930) Scottish
A Hind's Daughter
Oil on canvas: 91.5 x 76.2
Signed and dated 1883
Bequest of Sir James Lewis Caw 1951
NG 2142

Sir James GUTHRIE
(1859–1930) Scottish
Mrs Craig Sellar of Ardtornish (1844–1929)
Oil on canvas: 197 x 115.5
Signed and dated 1910
Bequest of Gerard Hay Craig Sellar 1930;
received 1954
NG 2176

Sir James GUTHRIE
(1859–1930) Scottish
The Velvet Cloak (Mrs Alexander Maitland)
Oil on canvas: 201 x 109
Signed
Bequest of Sir Alexander Maitland 1965
NG 2284

Sir James GUTHRIE
(1859–1930) Scottish
In a Monastery Garden
Oil on canvas: 27.7 x 34
Signed and dated 1884
Bequest of Dr Robert A. Lillie 1977
NG 2353

Sir James GUTHRIE
(1859–1930) Scottish
The Shepherd Boy
Oil on canvas: 54 x 77.5
Signed
Bequest of Dr Robert A. Lillie 1977
NG 2354

Noël HALLÉ
(1711–81) French
A Druids' Ceremony
Oil on canvas: 49.5 x 60
Purchased 1993
NG 2558

Frans HALS
(c. 1580/85–1666) Dutch
A Dutch Gentleman
Oil on canvas: 115 x 86.1
Presented by William McEwan 1885
NG 691

Frans HALS
(*c.* 1580/85–1666) Dutch
A Dutch Lady
Oil on canvas: 115 x 85.8
Presented by William McEwan 1885
NG 692

Frans HALS
(*c.* 1580/85–1666) Dutch
Verdonck
Oil on panel: 46.7 x 35.5
Signed in monogram
Presented by John J. Moubray of Naemoor 1916
NG 1200

Gavin HAMILTON
(1723–98) Scottish
Achilles Lamenting the Death of Patroclus
Oil on canvas: 227.3 x 391.2
Purchased 1976
NG 2339

Gavin HAMILTON
(1723–98) Scottish
Andromache Bewailing the Death of Hector
Oil on canvas: 64.2 x 98.5
Purchased with the aid of the Barrogill Keith
Bequest Fund 1985
NG 2428

Gawen HAMILTON
(*c.* 1697–1737) Scottish
Nicol Graham of Gartmore (1695–1775)
and Two Friends Seated in a Library
Oil on canvas: 63.5 x 60.5
Purchased 1988
NG 2464

Formerly attributed to James HAMILTON
(*c.* 1640– *c.* 1720)
Still Life
Oil on canvas: 47.8 x 40.5
With signature and date 1695
Purchased 1935
NG 1833

Henri HARPIGNIES
(1819–1916) French
The Banks of the Loire
Oil on canvas: 65.5 x 81.3
Signed
Bequest of Hugh A. Laird 1911
NG 1048

Henri HARPIGNIES
(1819–1916) French
Cliffs near Crémieu
Oil on canvas: 38 x 46
Signed and dated 1847
Purchased 1985
NG 2432

Sir George HARVEY
(1806–76) Scottish
The Covenanters' Communion
Oil on panel: 98.3 x 114
Signed
Presented by William Forrester to the RSA 1874;
transferred and presented 1910
NG 608

Sir George HARVEY
(1806–76) Scottish
The Schule Skailin'
Oil on panel: 71.7 x 121.8
Signed
Presented by Mrs Duncan J. Kay 1904
NG 919

Sir George HARVEY
(1806–76) Scottish
The Bowlers
Oil on canvas: 90.2 x 182
Signed and dated 1850
Presented by Sir Donald Currie 1907
NG 949

Sir George HARVEY
(1806–76) Scottish
Two Seated Men and a Standing Boy:
Study for 'The Covenanters' Baptism'
Oil on millboard with pencil underdrawing:
33.6 x 28
Bequest of Miss Ellen Harvey 1915
NG 1193 A

Sir George HARVEY
(1806–76) Scottish
*Four Standing Men: Study
for 'The Covenanters' Baptism'*
Oil on millboard with pencil underdrawing:
33.6 x 28
Bequest of Miss Ellen Harvey 1915
NG 1193 B

Sir George HARVEY
(1806–76) Scottish
*Two Seated Men: Study
for 'The Covenanters' Baptism'*
Oil on millboard with pencil underdrawing:
33.6 x 28
Inscribed
Bequest of Miss Ellen Harvey 1915
NG 1193 C

Sir George HARVEY
(1806–76) Scottish
*Two Men and a Girl Standing: Study
for 'The Covenanters' Baptism'*
Oil on millboard with pencil underdrawing:
33.6 x 28
Inscribed
Bequest of Miss Ellen Harvey 1915
NG 1193 D

Sir George HARVEY
(1806–76) Scottish
A Girl and Two Women Standing and Holding a Baby: Study for 'The Covenanters' Baptism'
Oil on millboard with pencil underdrawing:
33.6 x 28
Bequest of Miss Ellen Harvey 1915
NG 1193 E

Sir George HARVEY
(1806–76) Scottish
A Boy and a Girl with a Collie Dog Standing by a Stream: Study for 'The Covenanters' Baptism'
Oil on millboard with pencil underdrawing:
33.6 x 28
Inscribed
Bequest of Miss Ellen Harvey 1915
NG 1193 F

Sir George HARVEY
(1806–76) Scottish
Two Children: Study for 'Quitting the Manse'
(NG 2308)
Oil on millboard: 54.6 x 45.7
Presented by Mrs Ethel M. Pearse 1946
NG 2045

Sir George HARVEY
(1806–76) Scottish
Learning to Walk
Oil on panel: 40.6 x 58.7
Presented by Mrs Ethel M. Pearse 1947
NG 2089

Sir George HARVEY
(1806–76) Scottish
The Village School
Oil on panel: 42.2 x 58.5
Signed
Presented by Mrs Ethel M. Pearse 1947
NG 2090

Sir George HARVEY
(1806–76) Scottish
*Two Women and a Boy: Study
for 'The Covenanters Preaching'*
Oil on board: 33.6 x 26.3
Inscribed, signed in monogram and dated 1857
Presented by Mrs Ethel M. Pearse 1947
NG 2091

Sir George HARVEY
(1806–76) Scottish
*A Man with a Pike: Study
for 'The Covenanters Preaching'*
Oil on board: 32.4 x 26.7
Inscribed, signed in monogram and dated 1861
Presented by Mrs Ethel M. Pearse 1947
NG 2092

Sir George HARVEY
(1806–76) Scottish
*Quitting the Manse. An Incident in Forming
the Free Church of Scotland in 1843*
Oil on canvas: 152 x 244
Presented by Robert Horn and a group
of subscribers 1860
NG 2308 (formerly NG 383)

Sir George HARVEY
(1806–76) Scottish
The Curlers
Oil on panel: 55.8 x 167.7
Signed and dated 1835
Purchased 1995
NG 2641

Attributed to Sir George HARVEY
(1806–76) Scottish
The Curlers
Oil on canvas: 35.9 x 79.4
Purchased 1923
NG 1579

Jan Davidsz. de HEEM
(1605/6–1683/84) Dutch
Still Life with Fruit and Lobster
Oil on panel: 33.7 x 41.7
Signed and dated 1650
Bequest of Mrs Nisbet Hamilton Ogilvy
of Biel 1921
NG 1505

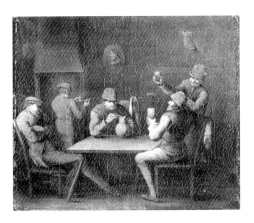

Follower of Egbert van HEEMSKERCK
(1634/35–1704) Dutch
Boors Carousing
Oil on canvas: 24.1 x 28.6
Bequest of Mrs Nisbet Hamilton Ogilvy
of Biel 1921
NG 1515

George HENRY
(1858–1943) Scottish
Barr, Ayrshire
Oil on panel: 22.5 x 30.5
Signed
Reverse: inscribed
Purchased 1978
NG 2361

George HENRY
(1858–1943) Scottish
East and West
Oil on canvas: 102 x 76.6
Signed
Bequest of Mr and Mrs G. D. Robinson through
the National Art Collections Fund 1988
NG 2454

George HENRY
(1858–1943) Scottish
Geisha Girl
Oil on canvas: 53.3 x 32.8
Inscribed, signed and dated 1894
Bequest of Alexander Esmé Gordon 1993
NG 2583

Robert HERDMAN
(1829–88) Scottish
After the Battle: A Scene in Covenanting Times
Oil on canvas: 115.8 x 173
Signed in monogram and dated 1870
Commissioned by RAPFAS 1870;
transferred 1897
NG 599

Robert HERDMAN
(1829–88) Scottish
Emily Merelina Meymott, Baroness Shand
(died 1911)
Oil on canvas: 221.8 x 146.6
Signed in monogram and dated 1867
Presented by Baroness Shand 1906
NG 934

Robert HERDMAN
(1829–88) Scottish
Evening Thoughts
Oil on millboard laid on canvas: 61 x 45.8
Signed in monogram and dated 1864 (indistinctly)
Presented by Mrs Annie Dunlop from
the estate of George B. Dunlop 1951
NG 2136

Robert HERDMAN
(1829–88) Scottish
Mary Queen of Scots' Farewell to France
Oil on canvas: 91.8 x 71.4
Signed in monogram and dated 1867
Bequest of Miss Mary Beatrice
Maude Herdman 1995
NG 2636

David Octavius HILL
(1802–70) Scottish
On the Quay at Leith
Oil on panel: 30 x 35.6
Purchased by the RI 1826; transferred 1859
NG 210

David Octavius HILL
(1802–70) Scottish
*Edinburgh Old and New (Edinburgh,
on the Queens Birthday, Viewed from the Mons
Meg Battery, Castle, News from India)*
Oil on panel: 117 x 193
Signed
Purchased 1942
NG 1964

Meindert HOBBEMA
(1638–1709) Dutch
A Waterfall in a Wood
Oil on panel: 26.9 x 22.3
Signed
Bequest of Mrs Nisbet Hamilton Ogilvy
of Biel 1921
NG 1506

Meindert HOBBEMA
(1638–1709) Dutch
Wooded Landscape
Oil on canvas: 93.7 x 130.8
Purchased with the aid of the National Art
Collections Fund and the National Heritage
Purchase Grant (Scotland) 1979
NG 2377

Meindert HOBBEMA
(1638–1709) Dutch
Landscape with a View of the Bergkerk, Deventer
Oil on panel: 38.6 x 53.3
Signed and dated 168[ ]
Lent by the Duke of Sutherland 1945

Attributed to David HODGSON
(1798–1864) English
A Heath: Sunset
Oil on canvas: 60.7 x 123.2
Presented by James Staat Forbes 1899
NG 844

William HOGARTH
(1697–1764) English
Sarah Malcolm (died 1733)
Oil on canvas: 48.8 x 38.7
Bequest of Lady Jane Dundas 1897
NG 838

After William HOGARTH
(1697–1764) English
*Gustavus Hamilton, 2nd Viscount Boyne
(1710–46)*
Oil on canvas: 50.8 x 37.8
Purchased with the aid of the Cowan Smith
Bequest Fund 1925
NG 1657

Hans HOLBEIN the Younger
(1497/98–1543) German
An Allegory of the Old and New Testaments
Oil on panel: 50 x 60.5
Purchased by Private Treaty with the aid of the
National Heritage Memorial Fund and the
National Heritage Purchase Grant (Scotland) 1981
NG 2407

James HOLLAND
(1800–70) English
The Rialto, Venice
Oil on canvas: 22.8 (circular)
Purchased 1909
NG 980

John HOPPNER
(1758–1810) English
*Admiral Adam Duncan, 1st Viscount Duncan
of Camperdown (1731–1804)*
Oil on canvas: 75.5 x 63.5
Bequest of the Earl of Camperdown 1918
NG 1216

Edward Atkinson HORNEL
(1864–1933) Scottish
The Music of the Woods
Oil on canvas: 121 x 151.1
Signed and dated 1906
Presented by Sir Hugh Reid 1934
NG 1814

Edward Atkinson HORNEL
(1864–1933) Scottish
Kite Flying, Japan
Oil on canvas: 76.2 x 48.5
Signed
Presented by Sir Hugh Reid 1934
NG 1815

Edward Atkinson HORNEL
(1864–1933) Scottish
A Girl and Goats
Oil on canvas: 39 x 32
Signed
Bequest of Sir James Lewis Caw 1951
NG 2145

Gerrit HOUCKGEEST
(c. 1600–61) Dutch
An Architectural Fantasy with Figures
Oil on canvas: 131.1 x 152
Signed and dated 1638
Purchased by the RI 1830; transferred 1859
NG 46

John HOUSTON
(1812–84) Scottish
A Curiosity Dealer
Oil on canvas: 60 x 48.5
Signed and dated 1845
Bequest of Patrick Shaw 1903
NG 914

Henry HOWARD
(1769–1847) English
Venus Carrying off Ascanius
Oil on canvas: 69.8 x 91.1
Purchased by the RI 1826; transferred 1859
NG 213

Thomas HUDSON
(1701–79) English
Charles Erskine (1716–49)
Oil on canvas: 75.5 x 62.2
Purchased 1950
NG 2131

Robert Gemmell HUTCHISON
(1855–1936) Scottish
Strawberries and Cream
Oil on canvas: 80.3 x 102.2
Presented by Mrs Ann Laidlaw 1974
NG 2333

Robert Gemmell HUTCHISON
(1855–1936) Scottish
The Young Arcadians
Oil on panel: 20.1 x 30.2
Reverse: with inscription
Bequest of Mrs Ann Laidlaw 1979
NG 2379

Cornelis HUYSMANS
(1648–1727) Flemish
Landscape with Cattle and Figures
Oil on canvas: 84.5 x 120.7
Presented to the RI by Robert Clouston 1852;
transferred 1859
NG 47

Hans HYSING
(1678– *c.* 1753) Swedish
Portrait of a Man, called Sir Peter Halkett,
2nd Bart of Pitfirrane (died 1755)
Oil on canvas: 74.5 x 62
Signed and dated 1735
Purchased 1951
NG 2159

Jozef ISRAËLS
(1824–1911) Dutch
Watching the Flock
Oil on panel: 29.8 x 42.6
Signed
Bequest of Hugh A. Laird 1911
NG 1059

Jozef ISRAËLS
(1824–1911) Dutch
Bringing Home the Calf
Oil on panel: 29.9 x 41.9
Signed
Bequest of Hugh A. Laird 1911
NG 1060

Jozef ISRAËLS
(1824–1911) Dutch
A Sea Urchin
Oil on panel: 25.4 x 19
Signed
Bequest of Hugh A. Laird 1911
NG 1061

ITALIAN School
(15th century)
St Francis Receiving the Stigmata
Panel: 38.5 x 24
Purchased 1930
NG 1745

ITALIAN School
(17th century)
A Battlefield: Trumpeters Sounding a Recall
Oil on canvas: 105.2 x 232
Presented by James S. Wardrop for the future
National Gallery 1850
NG 85

ITALIAN School
(17th century)
A Hermit Saint Doing Penance
Oil on canvas: 105.4 x 89.4
Presented by Henry Doig 1888
NG 812

ITALIAN School
(18th century)
Portrait of a Man
Oil on canvas: 81.5 x 61
Bequest of Sir Claude Phillips 1924
NG 1638

ITALIAN School
(18th or 19th century)
A City Square
Oil on canvas: 68 x 93.5
Bequest of Patrick Shaw 1903
NG 910

Charles JACQUE
(1813–94) French
Sheep at a Watering Place
Oil on canvas: 81.5 x 65.4
Signed
Bequest of Hugh A. Laird 1911
NG 1046

Charles JACQUE
(1813–94) French
Leaving the Stall
Oil on canvas: 46.6 x 67.5
Signed
Bequest of Dr John Kirkhope 1920
NG 1457

George JAMESONE
(1589/90–1644) Scottish
Mary Erskine, Countess Marischal (born c. 1597)
Oil on canvas: 67.3 x 54.6
Inscribed and dated 1626
Purchased 1908
NG 958

William Borthwick JOHNSTONE
(1804–68) Scottish
The Daughters of Thomas Duncan: Mary Helen
Duncan (born 1835) and Jane Duncan (born 1839)
Watercolour on ivory: 28.9 x 22.5 (unfinished)
Purchased 1930
NG 1749

After Jacob JORDAENS
(1593–1678) Flemish
Portrait of a Man
Oil on canvas: 96.7 x 76
Presented by Alexander Wood Inglis 1870
NG 579

Angelica KAUFFMANN
(1741–1807) Swiss
Michael Novosielski (1750–95)
Oil on canvas: 128 x 101.6
Inscribed, signed and dated 1791
Bequest of Mrs Elizabeth Stewart 1879
NG 651

Attributed to Willem KEY
(*c*. 1515–68) Netherlandish
Portrait of a Man, called Mark Ker (died 1584)
Oil on panel: 39.3 x 29
With inscription and date 1551
Bequest of the 11th Marquess of Lothian 1941
NG 1938

Attributed to Willem KEY
(*c*. 1515–68) Netherlandish
*Portrait of a Lady, called Lady Helen Leslie,
Wife of Mark Ker*
Oil on panel: 39.3 x 28.9
With inscription and date 1551
Bequest of the 11th Marquess of Lothian 1941
NG 1939

William KIDD
(1796–1863) Scottish
Fisher Folk
Oil on canvas: 30.5 x 41
Presented by Alexander Kellock Brown 1909
NG 982

William KIDD
(1796–1863) Scottish
Indulging
Oil on panel: 50 x 39.2
Signed and dated 1832
Purchased 1992
NG 2547

John KNOX
(1778–1845) Scottish
Landscape with Tourists at Loch Katrine
Oil on canvas: 90 x 125
Purchased 1992
NG 2557

Christen KØBKE
(1810–48) Danish
A View of the Square in the Kastel looking towards the Ramparts
Oil on canvas: 30 x 23.4
Purchased with the aid of the National Art Collections Fund 1989
NG 2505

Philips KONINCK
(1619–88) Dutch
Extensive Landscape
Oil on canvas: 91 x 111.8
Purchased by Private Treaty 1986
NG 2434

Nicolas LANCRET
(1690–1743) French
The Toy Windmill
Oil on canvas: 49.5 (circular)
Bequest of Lady Murray of Henderland 1861
NG 440

Sir Edwin LANDSEER
(1802–73) English
Rent-day in the Wilderness
Oil on canvas: 122 x 265
Bequest of Sir Roderick Murchison 1871
NG 586

James Eckford LAUDER
(1811–69) Scottish
Bailie Duncan McWheeble at Breakfast
(from Scott's 'Waverley')
Oil on canvas: 67.3 x 50.2
Signed and dated 1854
Bequest of Lady Dawson Brodie 1903
NG 915

James Eckford LAUDER
(1811–69) Scottish
James Watt and the Steam Engine:
the Dawn of the Nineteenth Century
Oil on canvas: 147.3 x 238.7
Signed in monogram
Purchased 1986
NG 2435

Robert Scott LAUDER
(1803–69) Scottish
Christ Teacheth Humility
Oil on canvas: 237.8 x 353
Purchased by RAPFAS 1849; transferred 1897
NG 221

Robert Scott LAUDER
(1803–69) Scottish
The Artist's Brother (Henry Lauder, 1807–27)
Oil on canvas: 75 x 62.3
Presented to the RSA after 1882 by Dr Scott
Lauder; transferred and presented 1910
NG 1003

Robert Scott LAUDER
(1803–69) Scottish
A Study for 'Christ Teacheth Humility' (NG 221)
Oil on canvas laid on board: 32.5 x 57.6
Purchased 1972
NG 2316

Robert Scott LAUDER
(1803–69) Scottish
*The Gow Chrom Reluctantly Conducting
the Glee Maiden to a Place of Safety (from Scott's
'The Fair Maid of Perth')*
Oil on canvas: 111.2 x 86
Signed and dated 1846
Purchased with the aid of the Barrogill Keith
Bequest Fund 1985
NG 2429

Sir John LAVERY
(1856–1941) Irish/Scottish
Loch Katrine
Oil on canvas: 63.2 x 76.2
Signed
Reverse: with inscription and date 1913
Presented by Mrs Annie Dunlop from the estate
of George B. Dunlop 1951
NG 2135

Sir John LAVERY
(1856–1941) Irish/Scottish
*The Dutch Cocoa House at the Glasgow
International Exhibition of 1888*
Oil on canvas: 45.8 x 35.7
Signed and dated 1888
Purchased with the aid of the Barrogill Keith
Bequest Fund 1985
NG 2431

Sir Thomas LAWRENCE
(1769–1830) English
Mary Digges, Lady Robert Manners (1737–1829)
Oil on canvas: 138.8 x 110.5
Bequest of Mrs Nisbet Hamilton Ogilvy
of Biel 1921
NG 1522

Cecil Gordon LAWSON
(1851–82) English
The Old Mill: Sunset
Oil on canvas: 104.8 x 135.2
Signed and dated 1881
Purchased 1908
NG 966

Cecil Gordon LAWSON
(1851–82) English
Surrey Landscape
Oil on panel: 30.5 x 25.4
Signed
Purchased 1920
NG 1372

Alphonse LEGROS
(1837–1911) French
The Sermon
Oil on canvas: 76.2 x 95.9
Signed and dated 1871
Purchased 1923
NG 1623

Sir Peter LELY
(1618–80) Dutch/English
Lady Diana Bruce, Duchess of Rutland (died 1672)
Oil on canvas: 122 x 96.5
Bequest of Mrs Nisbet Hamilton Ogilvy
of Biel 1921
NG 1507

Anicet-Charles-Gabriel LEMONNIER
(1743–1824) French
*St Charles Borromeo bringing the Assistance
of Religion to the Plague Victims of Milan*
Oil on canvas: 59 x 36
Purchased 1994
NG 2593

Franz von LENBACH
(1836–1904) German
Prince Otto von Bismarck (1815–98)
Oil on panel: 77.6 x 63.6
Presented by J. Kennedy Todd to the RSA 1903;
transferred and presented 1910
NG 916

After LEONARDO da Vinci
(1452–1519) Italian
The Madonna of the Yarnwinder
Oil on panel: 62 x 48.8
Presented by Captain Douglas Hope 1964
NG 2270

Stanislas LÉPINE
(1835–92) French
The Pont de l'Alma, Paris
Oil on canvas: 30.5 x 53.5
Signed
Bequest of Hugh A. Laird 1911
NG 1047

Stanislas LÉPINE
(1835–92) French
Sunset on a River
Oil on canvas: 26 x 33
Signed
Bequest of Dr John Kirkhope 1920
NG 1458

Attributed to Stanislas LÉPINE
(1835–92) French
Montmartre
Oil on canvas: 33.2 x 24.4
With studio stamp
Bequest of Dr John Kirkhope 1920
NG 1459

Imitator of Stanislas LÉPINE
(1835–92) French
Landscape with Farm Buildings
Oil on panel: 18 x 34.3
With signature
Bequest of Dr John MacGregor 1942
NG 1969

Jan LIEVENS
(1607–74) Dutch
Portrait of a Young Man
Oil on canvas: 112 x 99.4
Purchased with the aid of the Cowan Smith
Bequest Fund 1922
NG 1564

Filippino LIPPI
(*c.* 1457–1504) Italian
The Nativity with Two Angels
Panel: 25 x 37
Purchased 1931
NG 1758

William Home LIZARS
(1788–1859) Scottish
Reading the Will
Oil on panel: 51.5 x 64.8
Presented by Mrs Henrietta Lizars 1861
NG 423

William Home LIZARS
(1788–1859) Scottish
A Scotch Wedding
Oil on panel: 59.1 x 66
Presented by Mrs Henrietta Lizars 1861
NG 424

William Ewart LOCKHART
(1846–1900) Scottish
*Gil Blas and the Archbishop of Granada
(from Lesage's 'The Adventures of Gil Blas
de Santillane')*
Oil on canvas: 151 x 92.7
Signed and dated 1878
Purchased 1907
NG 945

LOMBARD School
(17th century)
Christ on the Mount of Olives
Oil on canvas: 91.4 x 179
Purchased by the RI 1830; transferred 1859
NG 60

Follower of LORENZO di Credi
(1456/59–1536) Italian
The Holy Family
Panel: 30 (circular)
Bequest of David Laing 1879
NG 646

LORENZO Monaco (Piero di Giovanni) and
Workshop
(before 1372–1422/24) Italian
The Virgin and Child
Tempera and gold on panel: 101.6 x 61.7
Purchased 1965
NG 2271

John Henry LORIMER
(1856–1936) Scottish
The Ordination of Elders in a Scottish Kirk
Oil on canvas: 109.2 x 140
Signed and dated 1891
Presented by Mrs McGrath to the Scottish Modern
Arts Association; received 1936
NG 1879

Lorenzo LOTTO
(c. 1480–1556/57) Italian
The Virgin and Child with St Jerome, St Peter,
St Francis and an Unidentified Female Saint
Oil on canvas transferred from panel: 82.5 x 105
Signed
Purchased by Private Treaty with the aid
of the National Heritage Memorial Fund 1984
NG 2418

Maximilien LUCE
(1858–1941) French
Lucie Cousturier (1876–1925) in her Garden
Oil on panel: 32.4 x 23.6
Signed
Bequest of Mrs Isabel M. Traill 1986
NG 2444

Simon LUTTICHUYS
(1610–62) Dutch
Still Life
Oil on canvas: 73.2 x 84
Signed with initials
Bequest of Mrs Nisbet Hamilton Ogilvy
of Biel 1921
NG 1504

Horatio McCULLOCH
(1805–67) Scottish
Inverlochy Castle
Oil on canvas: 91.6 x 152.8
Signed and dated 1857
Purchased by RAPFAS 1857; transferred 1897
NG 288

Horatio McCULLOCH
(1805–67) Scottish
A Lowland River
Oil on canvas: 99 x 150
Signed and dated 1851
Bequest of Robert Cox 1872
NG 587

Horatio McCULLOCH
(1805–67) Scottish
Hawthornden Castle
Oil on canvas laid on panel: 35.6 x 51
Signed
Bequest of Mr and Mrs G. D. Robinson through
the National Art Collections Fund 1988
NG 2456

Horatio McCULLOCH
(1805–67) Scottish
Highland Landscape with a Waterfall
Oil on canvas: 259.4 x 152.5
Purchased 1992
NG 2587

William Stewart MacGEORGE
(1861–1931) Scottish
A Galloway Peat Moss
Oil on canvas laid on panel: 81.2 x 134.6
Signed and dated 1888
Reverse: inscribed
Bequest of Dr Samuel Murdoch Riddick 1975
NG 2334

Robert McGREGOR
(1847/48–1922) Scottish
Great Expectations
Oil on canvas: 76 x 137.3
Signed and dated 1879
Purchased 1986
NG 2437

William York MACGREGOR
(1855–1923) Scottish
The Vegetable Stall
Oil on canvas: 106.7 x 153
Signed and dated 1884
Presented by Mrs William York MacGregor 1939
NG 1915

William York MACGREGOR
(1855–1923) Scottish
A Castle on a Cliff
Oil on canvas: 34.2 x 39.4
Signed and dated 1906
Bequest of Mrs William York MacGregor 1942
NG 1957

William York MACGREGOR
(1855–1923) Scottish
Winter Landscape
Oil on canvas: 92 x 81.5
Signed and dated 1908
Purchased 1947
NG 2086

William York MacGREGOR
(1855–1923) Scottish
A Rocky Solitude
Oil on canvas laid on board: 62.9 x 67.7
Signed and dated 1896
Presented by Sir Alexander and
Lady Maitland 1958
NG 2200

Robert McINNES
(1801–86) Scottish
Self-portrait
Oil on canvas: 76.2 x 63.5
Signed with initials and dated 1850
Reverse: inscribed
Purchased 1934
NG 1804

William Darling McKAY
(1844–1924) Scottish
Field Working in Spring: At the Potato Pits
Oil on canvas: 64.2 x 97.5
Signed
Presented by the Misses Stodart 1926
NG 1669

William Darling McKAY
(1844–1924) Scottish
Haymakers
Oil on canvas: 50.5 x 69.1
Signed with initials
Presented by the artist's executors 1934
NG 1799

William Darling McKAY
(1844–1924) Scottish
Green Landscape
Oil on canvas: 35.7 x 60.8
Presented by the artist's executors 1934
NG 1800

William Darling McKAY
(1844–1924) Scottish
The Nungate Bridge, Haddington
Oil on canvas: 78.4 x 110.3
Signed with initials
Purchased 1988
NG 2463

Charles Hodge MACKIE
(1862–1920) Scottish
'Belvedere', Venice
Oil on canvas: 69.2 x 88.3
Signed and dated 1910
Bequest of Alexander F. Roberts 1929
NG 1732

Charles Hodge MACKIE
(1862–1920) Scottish
The Bathing Pool
Oil on canvas: 152 x 150
With signature
Presented by Mrs Charles Mackie 1946
NG 2038

Charles Hodge MACKIE
(1862–1920) Scottish
Entrance to the Grand Canal, Venice
Oil on canvas: 81.3 x 100.3
Signed
Purchased 1946
NG 2044

Thomas Hope McLACHLAN
(1845–97) Scottish
Christobel under the Oak
Oil on canvas: 61.6 x 94.6
Signed
Bequest of Thomas Hope McLachlan;
received from his widow Mrs H. P. Fry 1938
NG 1892

Sir Daniel MACNEE
(1806–82) Scottish
Horatio McCulloch (1805–67)
Oil on canvas: 75 x 62.2
Signed and dated 1858
Presented by the artist to the RSA 1859;
transferred and presented 1910
NG 610

Sir Daniel MACNEE
(1806–82) Scottish
*A Lady in Grey (Portrait of the Artist's Daughter,
later Mrs Wiseman)*
Oil on canvas: 128 x 102.5
Signed and dated 1859
Presented by Lady Macnee 1927
NG 1679

Sir Daniel MACNEE
(1806–82) Scottish
*A Portrait Study of a Gentleman Standing
in an Interior*
Oil on millboard: 52.3 x 31.7
Purchased 1935
NG 1817 A

Sir Daniel MACNEE
(1806–82) Scottish
*A Portrait Study of a Gentleman Seated
in an Interior*
Oil on millboard: 55.2 x 37
Purchased 1935
NG 1817 B

Sir Daniel MACNEE
(1806–82) Scottish
*A Portrait Study of a Gentleman Standing
in an Interior*
Oil on millboard: 52.3 x 32
Purchased 1935
NG 1817 C

Sir Daniel MACNEE
(1806–82) Scottish
*A Portrait Study of a Gentleman Seated
in an Interior*
Oil on millboard: 45.6 x 30
Purchased 1935
NG 1818 A

Sir Daniel MACNEE
(1806–22) Scottish
*A Portrait Study of a Gentleman Standing
in an Interior*
Oil on millboard: 45.6 x 30
Purchased 1935
NG 1818 B

Sir Daniel MACNEE
(1806–82) Scottish
A Portrait Study of Two Children in a Landscape
Reverse: *Study of a Young Man in an Interior* (see
next item)
Oil on millboard: 29.5 x 22
Signed with initials
Purchased 1935
NG 1819 A

Sir Daniel MACNEE
(1806–82) Scottish
Study of a Young Man in an Interior
Reverse of NG 1819 A

Sir Daniel MACNEE
(1806–82) Scottish
*A Portrait Study of a Lady and a Child
in an Interior*
Oil on millboard: 29.5 x 24.6
Purchased 1935
NG 1819 B

Sir Daniel MACNEE
(1806–82) Scottish
A Portrait Study of a Lady Seated in a Landscape
Oil on millboard: 29.5 x 22.3
Purchased 1935
NG 1819 C

Sir Daniel MACNEE
(1806–82) Scottish
A Portrait Study of Three Ladies and a Boy in Highland Dress in an Interior
Oil on millboard: 55.7 x 39.2
Purchased 1935
NG 1820

Sir Daniel MACNEE
(1806–82) Scottish
A Portrait Study of a Lady and Child in an Interior
Oil on millboard: 29.2 x 24.2
Purchased 1935
NG 1821

Sir Daniel MACNEE
(1806–82) Scottish
Sir James Bain (1817–98)
Oil on millboard: 35.2 x 25.2
Purchased 1935
NG 1822

Sir Daniel MACNEE
(1806–82) Scottish
*Louisa Balfour, Mrs James Mackenzie
of Craigpath*
Oil on canvas: 207 x 141
Signed
Presented by Mrs James Mackenzie 1940
NG 1921

Sir Daniel MACNEE
(1806–82) Scottish
A Lady
Oil on millboard: 31.1 x 25.4
Bequest of Kenneth Sanderson 1943; transferred
from the Department of Prints and Drawings 1958
NG 2201

Sir Daniel MACNEE
(1806–82) Scottish
A Study for 'A Lady in Grey' (NG 1679)
Oil on millboard: 28.3 x 23.1
Signed with initials
Presented by Miss Gertrude Hermes 1962
NG 2254

Bessie MacNICOL
(1869–1904) Scottish
Portrait of a Lady ('Phyllis in Town')
Oil on panel: 35.5 x 24.8
Signed and dated 1904
Presented by Mrs Isabel M. Traill 1979
NG 2393

William McTAGGART
(1835–1910) Scottish
The Coming of St Columba
Oil on canvas: 131 x 206
Signed and dated 1895
Purchased 1911
NG 1071

William McTAGGART
(1835–1910) Scottish
Mrs Leiper
Oil on canvas: 74.6 x 62.2
Signed and dated 1872
Bequest of William Leiper 1916
NG 1201

William McTAGGART
(1835–1910) Scottish
The Young Fishers
Oil on canvas: 72.4 x 108
Signed and dated 1876
Bequest of Dr John Kirkhope 1920
NG 1482

William McTAGGART
(1835–1910) Scottish
By Summer Seas
Oil on canvas: 44.4 x 64.8
Signed and dated 1890 – 96
Bequest of Dr John Kirkhope 1920
NG 1483

William McTAGGART
(1835–1910) Scottish
Molly (Mary Gavin, 1870–1942)
Oil on canvas: 99 x 63.5
Signed
Presented by Mrs L. Pilkington 1925
NG 1659

William McTAGGART
(1835–1910) Scottish
The Sailing of the Emigrant Ship
Oil on canvas: 77 x 87.5
Signed and dated 1895
Presented by Sir James Lewis Caw
and Lady Caw 1931
NG 1757

William McTAGGART
(1835–1910) Scottish
The Storm
Oil on canvas: 122 x 183
Signed and dated 1890
Presented by Mrs Andrew Carnegie 1935
NG 1834

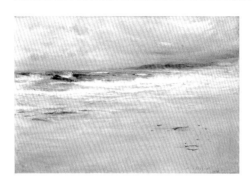

William McTAGGART
(1835–1910) Scottish
Machrihanish Bay
Oil on canvas: 82.5 x 123.2
Signed and dated 1878
Presented by Mr and Mrs D. W. T. Cargill 1938
NG 1906

William McTAGGART
(1835–1910) Scottish
Harvest at Broomieknowe
Oil on canvas: 87.3 x 130
Signed and dated 1896
Presented by Mr and Mrs D. W. T. Cargill 1938
NG 1907

William McTAGGART
(1835–1910) Scottish
Spring
Oil on canvas: 45.1 x 60.4
Signed in monogram and dated 1864
Bequest of Sir James Lewis Caw 1951
NG 2137

William McTAGGART
(1835–1910) Scottish
Snow in April
Oil on panel: 19.7 x 28.6
Signed
Bequest of Sir James Lewis Caw 1951
NG 2138

William McTAGGART
(1835–1910) Scottish
The Past and the Present ('The Builders')
Oil on canvas: 22.3 x 27.4
Bequest of Sir James Lewis Caw 1951
NG 2139

William McTAGGART
(1835–1910) Scottish
Quiet Sunset, Machrihanish
Oil on canvas: 38 x 45.9
Bequest of Sir James Lewis Caw 1951
NG 2140

William McTAGGART
(1835–1910) Scottish
Mrs William Lawrie
Oil on canvas: 90.8 x 60.4
Signed in monogram and dated 1881
Presented by Madame Violante Lawrie 1952
NG 2158

William McTAGGART
(1835–1910) Scottish
A Study of Oak Leaves in Autumn (Self-portrait)
Oil on canvas: 83.8 x 71.2
Signed and dated 1892
Presented by the William McTaggart Trust 1956
NG 2185

William McTAGGART
(1835–1910) Scottish
*The Artist's Mother (Barbara Brodie or Brolochan,
Mrs Dugald McTaggart, died 1884)*
Oil on canvas: 92.5 x 68.1
Presented by the William McTaggart Trust 1956
NG 2186

William McTAGGART
(1835–1910) Scottish
The Sailor's Yarn
Oil on canvas laid on board: 15.8 x 13.3
Bequest of Sir James Lewis Caw 1951
NG 2214

William McTAGGART
(1835–1910) Scottish
Halfway Home
Oil on canvas: 72 x 54.5
Signed and dated 1869
Bequest of Dr Robert A. Lillie 1977
NG 2355

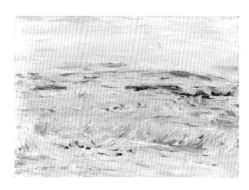

William McTAGGART
(1835–1910) Scottish
Harvest Moon
Oil on panel: 17.4 x 25.2
Bequest of Dr Robert A. Lillie 1977
NG 2356

William McTAGGART
(1835–1910) Scottish
A Study of Two Female Nude Models
Oil on canvas: 61 x 58
Purchased 1981
NG 2411

William McTAGGART
(1835–1910) Scottish
The Bait Gatherers
Oil on canvas: 66 x 84
Signed and dated 1879
Bequest of Thomas Godfrey Kirkness 1982
NG 2415

William McTAGGART
(1835–1910) Scottish
Autumn Evening, Broomieknowe
Oil on canvas: 102.7 x 164.4
Purchased 1990
NG 2511

William McTAGGART
(1835–1910) Scottish
*'The Belle' (The Artist's Daughter,
Jean Isobel McTaggart, 1880–1955)*
Oil on canvas: 151 x 91
Signed in monogram and dated 1886
Bequest of Miss Jean Isobel McTaggart 1955;
received 1991
NG 2528

William McTAGGART
(1835–1910) Scottish
A Life Study of a Seated Nude Male Model
Oil on paper laid on board: 48.5 x 36.3
Purchased 1994
NG 2637

William McTAGGART
(1835–1910) Scottish
A Life Study of a Standing Nude Male Model
Oil on paper laid on board: 55 x 38.5
Purchased 1994
NG 2638

William McTAGGART
(1835–1910) Scottish
*A Life Study of a Female Nude Model Seated
on White Drapery*
Oil on paper laid on board: 54.4 x 38.5
Purchased 1994
NG 2639

William McTAGGART
(1835–1910) Scottish
A Life Study of a Female Nude Model
with her Left Arm Raised
Oil on paper laid on board: 54 x 34.5
Purchased 1994
NG 2640

Nicolaes MAES
(1634–93) Dutch
A Dutch Family Group
Oil on panel: 50.5 x 38 (arched)
Bequest of Mrs Nisbet Hamilton Ogilvy
of Biel 1921
NG 1509

Imitator of Edouard MANET
(1832–83) French
Still Life
Oil on canvas: 36.8 x 45.1
With signature
Purchased 1923
NG 1618

Emile van MARCKE
(1827–90) French
Grazing Cattle
Oil on canvas: 61.3 x 66.3
Signed
Bequest of Hugh A. Laird 1911
NG 1054

Emile van MARCKE
(1827–90) French
The Pond on the Common
Oil on canvas: 45.3 x 60
Signed
Bequest of Hugh A. Laird 1911
NG 1055

Jacob MARIS
(1837–99) Dutch
On the Amstel
Oil on canvas: 94 x 125.4
Signed
Bequest of Hugh A. Laird 1911
NG 1049

Jacob MARIS
(1837–99) Dutch
Amsterdam
Oil on canvas: 34.3 x 58.4
Signed
Bequest of Hugh A. Laird 1911
NG 1050

Jacob MARIS
(1837–99) Dutch
Scheveningen
Oil on canvas: 43.8 x 30.2
Signed
Bequest of Hugh A. Laird 1911
NG 1051

Jacob MARIS
(1837–99) Dutch
Outside a Café
Oil on panel: 28 x 21.5
Signed
Bequest of Hugh A. Laird 1911
NG 1052

Jacob MARIS
(1837–99) Dutch
The Watermill, Bougival
Oil on panel: 15.2 x 21
Signed and dated 1871
Bequest of Dr John Kirkhope 1920
NG 1471

Willem MARIS
(1844–1910) Dutch
A Silver Stream
Oil on canvas: 47 x 37.5
Signed
Bequest of Hugh A. Laird 1911
NG 1053

William MARLOW
(1740–1813) English
A Town and Castle on a River
Oil on canvas: 81.3 x 114.7
Bequest of Lady Murray of Henderland 1861
NG 431

Francesco MARMITTA
(*c.* 1462/66–1505) Italian
*The Scourging of Christ with St Jerome
and St Benedict*
Panel: 35.8 x 25
Purchased 1927
NG 1673

David MARTIN
(1737–97) Scottish
Self-portrait
Oil on canvas: 49.5 x 39.4
Presented by the artist's relatives, the Misses
Bryce, to the RSA; transferred and presented 1910
NG 569

David MARTIN
(1737–97) Scottish
Lillias Seton, Lady Steuart of Allanton (died 1821)
Oil on canvas: 125.7 x 100.5
Signed and dated 1789
Presented by Sir Douglas Seton-Steuart 1928
NG 1718

Attributed to David MARTIN
(1737–97) Scottish
Mary Martin, Mrs Alexander Gowan (1716–95)
Oil on canvas: 86 x 71.5
Presented by Miss Jane Gowan 1940
NG 1926

John MARTIN
(1789–1854) English
Macbeth
Oil on canvas: 50.1 x 71
Purchased 1949
NG 2115

Quentin MASSYS
(1465/66–1530) Netherlandish
Portrait of a Man
Oil on panel: 80 x 64.5
Accepted in lieu of tax 1965
NG 2273

MASTER of the ADIMARI CASSONE
(active mid-15th century) Italian
The Triumph of a Roman General
Tempera, gold and silver on canvas, transferred
from panel: 40.5 x 70.5
Purchased 1942
NG 1975

MASTER of the FEMALE HALF-LENGTHS
(active *c.* 1530) Netherlandish
St Mary Magdalene Reading
Oil on panel: 38.7 x 25.5
Accepted in lieu of tax by the National Trust
for Scotland 1958; transferred by H. M. Treasury
to the National Galleries of Scotland 1984
NG 2427

MASTER of the SAN LUCCHESE
ALTARPIECE
(active mid-14th century) Italian
A Baptism
Tempera and gold on panel: 18.6 x 31.8
Purchased 1921
NG 1539 A

MASTER of the SAN LUCCHESE
ALTARPIECE
(active mid-14th century) Italian
A Martyrdom
Tempera and gold on panel: 18.6 x 29.6
Purchased 1921
NG 1539 B

MASTER of 1419
(active 1419) Italian
St Francis Receiving the Stigmata
Tempera and gold on panel: 21.6 x 30.5
Purchased 1921
NG 1540 A

MASTER of 1419
(active 1419) Italian
*St Anthony Abbot Exorcising a Woman Possessed
by the Devil*
Tempera and gold on panel: 21.6 x 30.5
Purchased 1921
NG 1540 B

MATTEO di Giovanni
(active 1452 – died 1495) Italian
The Virgin and Child with St Sebastian,
St Francis and Angels
Tempera and gold on panel. 51.3 x 39.7
Purchased 1910
NG 1023

Anton MAUVE
(1838–88) Dutch
The Tow-path: No. 1
Oil on canvas: 33 x 23.5
Signed
Bequest of Hugh A. Laird 1911
NG 1056

Anton MAUVE
(1838–88) Dutch
Field Labour
Oil on panel: 25.1 x 18.1
Signed
Bequest of Hugh A. Laird 1911
NG 1057

Anton MAUVE
(1838–88) Dutch
The Tow-path: No. 2
Oil on panel: 25 x 18
Signed
Bequest of Hugh A. Laird 1911
NG 1058

Sir John Baptiste de MEDINA
(*c.* 1659–1710) Flemish/Scottish
Portrait of a Young Man (probably the Artist's
Son, John Medina the Younger, 1721–96)
Oil on canvas: 77 x 63.5
Presented by Robert Chambers *c.* 1859
NG 305

John MEDINA the Younger
(1721–96) Flemish/Scottish
Copy of a Portrait of a Man (formerly called
John Scougall) (NG 2032)
Oil on canvas: 64.8 x 50.8
Bequest of John Scougall 1867
NG 554

Arthur MELVILLE
(1855–1904) Scottish
Christmas Eve: 'And there was no room for them in the inn'
Oil on canvas: 191 x 203 (unfinished)
Purchased 1907
NG 948

Arthur MELVILLE
(1855–1904) Scottish
An Arab Interior
Oil on canvas: 95 x 72.8
Inscribed, signed and dated 1881
Bequest of Sir James Lewis Caw 1951
NG 2144

Philippe MERCIER
(1689–1760) French
A Girl Holding a Cat
Oil on canvas: 91.4 x 70.5
Signed in monogram
Bequest of Lady Murray of Henderland 1861
NG 433

Philippe MERCIER
(1689–1760) French
A Girl Knitting
Oil on canvas: 76.2 x 63.5
Bequest of Lady Murray of Henderland 1861
NG 434

Philippe MERCIER
(1689–1760) French
Mr Dawson
Oil on canvas: 90.2 x 67.3
Bequest of the Revd Henry Humble 1877
NG 627

Philippe MERCIER
(1689–1760) French
Mrs Dawson
Oil on canvas: 90.2 x 67.3
Bequest of the Revd Henry Humble 1877
NG 628

Style of Philippe MERCIER
(1689–1760) French
A Boy and a Dog
Oil on canvas: 55.8 x 70.5
Bequest of C. J. G. Paterson 1942
NG 1961

Style of Philippe MERCIER
(1689–1760) French
A Girl with a Tea-cup
Oil on canvas: 55.8 x 70.5
Bequest of C. J. G. Paterson 1942
NG 1962

Conrad MEYER
(1618–68) Swiss
*Elisabeth Locher, Wife of Hans Konrad Heidegger
(1616–73)*
Oil on canvas: 73.5 x 57.5
Inscribed and dated 1661
Purchased 1887
NG 794

Achille-Etna MICHALLON
(1796–1822) French
A Study of a Tree
Oil on paper laid on canvas: 51 x 35
Purchased 1994
NG 2591

Georges MICHEL
(1763–1843) French
The Lime Kiln
Oil on canvas: 55 x 70
Presented by George R. MacDougall 1911
NG 1028

Georges MICHEL
(1763–1843) French
Montmartre
Oil on panel: 20.8 x 31.5
Bequest of Dr John Kirkhope 1920
NG 1461

Circle of Daniel MIJTENS the Elder
(1590– before 1648) Dutch
Portrait of a Man (formerly called John Scougall)
Oil on canvas: 62.3 x 50.2
Purchased 1945
NG 2032

Sir John Everett MILLAIS
(1829–96) English
'Sweetest eyes were ever seen'
Oil on canvas: 100.5 x 72
Signed in monogram and dated 1881
Bequest of Melville J. Gray 1946
NG 2067

William MILLAR
(active 1751–84) Scottish
Thomas Trotter
Oil on canvas: 73.7 x 62.2
Reverse: with inscription, signed and dated 1767
Purchased 1933
NG 1802

Hendrik van MINDERHOUT
(1632–96) Dutch
*An Engagement between the English
and the Dutch Fleets*
Oil on canvas: 73 x 125
Presented by George H. Girle 1860
NG 376

Follower of Pier Francesco MOLA
(1612–66) Italian
St Jerome
Oil on canvas: 61 x 79
Purchased by the RI 1830; transferred 1859
NG 29

Claude MONET
(1840–1926) French
Poplars on the Epte
Oil on canvas: 81.8 x 81.3
Signed
Purchased 1925
NG 1651

Claude MONET
(1840–1926) French
Haystacks, Snow Effect
Oil on canvas: 65 x 92
Signed and dated 1891
Bequest of Sir Alexander Maitland 1965
NG 2283

Claude MONET
(1840–1926) French
The Church at Vétheuil
Oil on canvas: 65.2 x 55.7
Signed and dated 1878
Presented by Mrs Isabel M. Traill 1979
NG 2385

Claude MONET
(1840–1926) French
A Seascape, Shipping by Moonlight
Oil on canvas: 60 x 73.8
Purchased 1980
NG 2399

Claude MONET
(1840–1926) French
Boats in a Harbour
Oil on canvas: 71.2 x 54
Signed
Bequest of Lord Amulree 1984
NG 2423

Francesco MONTI
(1685–1767) Italian
Rebecca at the Well
Oil on canvas: 78.7 x 84.5
Bequest of Miss Ida M. Hayward 1950
NG 2120

Adolphe-Joseph MONTICELLI
(1824–86) French
A Gypsy Encampment
Oil on panel: 21.6 x 46
Purchased 1908
NG 961

Adolphe-Joseph MONTICELLI
(1824–86) French
The Fête
Oil on panel: 39.8 x 59.5
Purchased 1910
NG 1022

Adolphe-Joseph MONTICELLI
(1824–86) French
The Garden of Love
Oil on panel: 39.2 x 59.7
Bequest of Dr John Kirkhope 1920
NG 1462

Adolphe-Joseph MONTICELLI
(1824–86) French
A Woodland Fête
Oil on panel: 26.5 x 45
Bequest of Dr John Kirkhope 1920
NG 1463

Adolphe-Joseph MONTICELLI
(1824–86) French
A Garden Fête
Oil on panel: 33.5 x 61
Bequest of Dr John Kirkhope 1920
NG 1464

Adolphe-Joseph MONTICELLI
(1824–86) French
In the Grotto
Oil on panel: 35 x 55
Signed
Bequest of Dr John Kirkhope 1920
NG 1465

Adolphe-Joseph MONTICELLI
(1824–86) French
Elegant Ladies in a Forest Clearing
Oil on canvas laid on panel: 37.2 x 25
Signed
Presented by Mrs Isabel M. Traill 1979
NG 2390

Adolphe-Joseph MONTICELLI
(1824–86) French
Fête Champêtre
Oil on panel: 40 x 59
Signed
Presented by Mrs Isabel M. Traill 1979
NG 2391

Albert MOORE
(1841–93) English
Beads
Oil on canvas: 29.8 x 51.6
Signed with a cipher and dated 1875
Purchased 1910
NG 1019

Jacob MORE
(1740–93) Scottish
Mount Vesuvius in Eruption ('The Last Days of Pompeii')
Oil on canvas: 151 x 201
Inscribed, signed and dated 1780
Presented to the RI by Sir James Steuart of Allanbank 1829; transferred 1859
NG 290

Jacob MORE
(1740–93) Scottish
The Falls of Clyde (Cora Linn)
Oil on canvas: 79.4 x 100.4
With inscription
Bequest of James Ramsay MacDonald 1938
NG 1897

Jacob MORE
(1740–93) Scottish
The Penitent St Mary Magdalene in a Landscape
Oil on panel: 30 x 38.1
Purchased 1990
NG 2518

Paulus MOREELSE
(1571–1638) Dutch
A Shepherd with a Pipe
Oil on canvas: 94.8 x 72.7
Purchased by the RI 1831; transferred 1859
NG 52

Paulus MOREELSE
(1571–1638) Dutch
Cimon and Pero
Oil on canvas: 147.5 x 162
Signed and dated 1633
Presented by Alexander Wood Inglis 1909
NG 1024

Berthe MORISOT
(1841–95) French
A Woman and Child in a Garden
Oil on canvas: 60 x 73.4
Signed
Purchased 1964
NG 2269

George MORLAND
(1763–1804) English
Selling Fish
Oil on canvas: 60.3 x 50.2
Signed and dated 179[1]
Presented by George R. MacDougall 1909
NG 993

George MORLAND
(1763–1804) English
Fighting Dogs
Oil on canvas: 64 x 82
Presented by W. B. Paterson 1909
NG 994

George MORLAND
(1763–1804) English
The Comforts of Industry
Oil on canvas: 31.5 x 37.6
Presented by Alexander and Lady Margaret Shaw,
later Lord and Lady Craigmyle, 1935
NG 1835

George MORLAND
(1763–1804) English
The Miseries of Idleness
Oil on canvas: 31.6 x 37.3
Presented by Alexander and Lady Margaret Shaw,
later Lord and Lady Craigmyle, 1935
NG 1836

George MORLAND
(1763–1804) English
The Public House Door
Oil on canvas: 62.9 x 77.5
Signed and dated 1792
Presented by Lord and Lady Craigmyle 1944
NG 2015

Imitator of George MORLAND
(1763–1804) English
The Stable Door
Oil on canvas: 31 x 36.8
With signature
Purchased 1887
NG 789

Giovanni Battista MORONI
(1520/24 – 1578) Italian
Giovanni Bressani (died 1560)
Oil on canvas: 116.2 x 88.8
Inscribed, signed and dated 1562
Purchased by Private Treaty 1977
NG 2347

William MOSMAN
(c. 1700–71) Scottish
Elizabeth Drummond, Mrs James Stuart
Oil on canvas: 82 x 66.7
Signed and dated 1740
Presented by M. V. Erskine Stuart 1930
NG 1752

Frederick de MOUCHERON
(1633–86) Dutch
Landscape with Travellers and a Herdsman
Oil on canvas: 120.5 x 105 (painted area)
Signed and dated 1677
Bequest of Patrick Shaw 1903
NG 909

David MUIRHEAD
(1867–1930) Scottish
Portrait of a Lady
Oil on canvas: 74 x 61.6
Signed and dated 1923
Presented by James Muirhead 1931
NG 1765

David MUIRHEAD
(1867–1930) Scottish
English Landscape
Oil on canvas: 42 x 51.7
Signed
Presented by James Muirhead 1934
NG 1801

David MUIRHEAD
(1867–1930) Scottish
Landscape with Figures
Oil on canvas: 61.3 x 92
Signed and dated 1911
Bequest of Mrs Mary Muirhead 1947
NG 2382

William MÜLLER
(1812–45) English
A Heath Scene
Oil on panel: 26 x 37.5
Signed and dated 1843
Bequest of Lady Binning 1952
NG 2166

Sir David MURRAY
(1849–1933) Scottish
Loch Coruisk, Skye
Oil on canvas: 70.5 x 90
Signed and dated 1874
Presented by Donald Fraser 1937
NG 1886

John James NAPIER
(1831–82) Scottish
*The First Lesson (The Artist's Wife, Janet Parker
Vance Langmuir with their Children, Janet
and James)*
Oil on canvas: 142 x 88.5
Bequest of Miss Barbara L. Napier 1991
NG 2541

Alexander NASMYTH
(1758–1840) Scottish
A Distant View of Stirling
Oil on canvas: 83.9 x 116.9
Commissioned by the RI in 1826; transferred 1859
NG 291

Alexander NASMYTH
(1758–1840) Scottish
The Windings of the Forth
Oil on canvas: 45.7 x 73.7
Presented by R. K. Blair 1920
NG 1383

Alexander NASMYTH
(1758–1840) Scottish
Wooded Landscape with Figures and Sheep
Oil on panel: 45 x 57.8
Presented by Frederick John Nettlefold 1948
NG 2100

Alexander NASMYTH
(1758–1840) Scottish
Edinburgh Castle and the Nor' Loch
Oil on canvas: 45.4 x 61
Signed
Reverse: inscribed and dated 182[4]
Presented by Mrs E. Pringle 1948
NG 2104

Alexander NASMYTH
(1758–1840) Scottish
*Princes Street with the Commencement
of the Building of the Royal Institution*
Oil on canvas: 122.5 x 165.5
Inscribed, signed and dated 1825
Presented by Sir David Baird 1991
NG 2542

Alexander NASMYTH
(1758–1840) Scottish
A View of Tivoli
Oil on canvas: 138 x 216
Purchased 1992
NG 2546

Alexander NASMYTH
(1758–1840) Scottish
A View of Tantallon Castle with the Bass Rock
Oil on canvas: 92 x 122.3
Inscribed and signed with initials
Purchased with the aid of the National Art
Collections Fund 1994
NG 2627

Charlotte NASMYTH
(1804–84) Scottish
Pastoral Landscape
Oil on canvas: 38.7 x 52
Purchased 1938
NG 1893

Elizabeth NASMYTH
(1793–1862) Scottish
The Falls of Clyde
Oil on canvas: 44.4 x 58.7
Purchased 1939
NG 1912

Patrick NASMYTH
(1787–1831) Scottish
English Landscape
Oil on canvas: 36.5 x 51
Signed and dated 1830
Purchased 1938
NG 1894

Patrick NASMYTH
(1787–1831) Scottish
Landscape
Oil on panel: 22.8 x 28
Signed
Bequest of Miss Alice Anne White 1941
NG 1948

Patrick NASMYTH
(1787–1831) Scottish
Wooded Landscape
Oil on panel: 21.6 x 29.8
Signed with initials
Bequest of Dr John MacGregor 1942
NG 1968

Patrick NASMYTH
(1787–1831) Scottish
A Scene in Hampshire
Oil on canvas: 22.2 x 30.5
Signed
Bequest of J. Cathcart White 1943
NG 1981

Patrick NASMYTH
(1787–1831) Scottish
A Woodman's Cottage
Oil on panel: 41.6 x 55.9
Signed and dated 182[0]
Presented by Frederick John Nettlefold 1948
NG 2101

Patrick NASMYTH
(1787–1831) Scottish
The Valley of the Tweed
Oil on canvas: 80.5 x 113.5
Reverse: with inscription
Presented by Frederick John Nettlefold 1948
NG 2102

Attributed to Patrick NASMYTH
(1787–1831) Scottish
Glenshira
Oil on canvas: 71 x 91.5
Presented by R. Murdoch Smith 1885
NG 589

Pieter NASON
(1612–88/90) Dutch
Portrait of a Couple
Oil on canvas: 135 x 147.3
Signed
Purchased by the RI 1840; transferred 1859
NG 117

NETHERLANDISH School
(15th century)
The Adoration of the Shepherds
Oil on panel: 67.3 x 106.6
Purchased 1921
NG 1541

NETHERLANDISH School
(16th century)
Bacchus and Ariadne
Oil on panel: 104 x 120.3
Purchased by the RI 1830; transferred 1859
NG 78

NETHERLANDISH School
(16th century)
Landscape: Midday
Oil on panel: 37.2 x 200.2 (painted area)
Purchased by the RI 1830; transferred 1859
NG 101

NETHERLANDISH School
(16th century)
The Emperor Charles V (1500–58) as a Child
Oil on panel: 19.5 x 14.5
Purchased 1920
NG 1254

NETHERLANDISH School
(16th century)
Derick Anthony (fl. 1550–69)
Oil on panel: 90.5 x 67.4
Inscribed and dated 1565
Bequest of Mrs Nisbet Hamilton Ogilvy
of Biel 1921
NG 1544

NETHERLANDISH School
(16th century)
Pietà
Oil on panel: 21.6 x 27.8
Purchased 1925
NG 1642

NETHERLANDISH School
(16th century)
Portrait of a Man, called James IV (1488–1513)
Oil on panel: 36.5 x 29.3
Bequest of the 11th Marquess of Lothian 1941
NG 1929

NETHERLANDISH School
(16th century)
The Virgin and Child
Oil on panel: 65 x 50.8
Purchased 1946
NG 2074

Albert NEUHUIJS
(1844–1914) Dutch
The Old, Old Story
Oil on canvas: 32.4 x 43.2
Signed
Bequest of Dr John Kirkhope 1920
NG 1473

Albert NEUHUIJS
(1844–1914) Dutch
Busy
Oil on canvas: 98 x 81.3
Signed
Bequest of Dr John Kirkhope 1920
NG 1474

Erskine NICOL
(1825–1904) Scottish
An Irish Emigrant Landing at Liverpool
Oil on canvas: 142 x 101
Signed and dated 1871
Presented by Sir A. Oliver Riddell 1905
NG 925

Pollock Sinclair NISBET
(1848–1922) Scottish
The Souk
Oil on canvas laid on board: 17.7 x 26.7
Signed and dated 1889
Reverse: with inscription
Bequest of Mr and Mrs G. D. Robinson through
the National Art Collections Fund 1988
NG 2458

James Campbell NOBLE
(1846–1913) Scottish
Sunset near Glencaple on Solway
Oil on canvas: 71 x 91.4
Signed
Presented by the artist's friends through
Robert Duddingstone Herdman 1914
NG 1146

Robert NOBLE
(1857–1917) Scottish
Springtime, Prestonkirk
Oil on canvas: 74 x 90
Signed and dated 1909
Presented by a body of subscribers through
William Miller Frazer 1917
NG 1208

James NORIE
(1684–1757) Scottish
Classical Landscape with Architecture
Oil on canvas: 68 x 136
Inscribed, signed and dated 1736
Purchased 1931
NG 1768

James NORIE
(1684–1757) Scottish
Classical Landscape with Trees and a Lake
Oil on canvas: 64.8 x 132
Inscribed, signed and dated 1736
Purchased 1931
NG 1769

John OPIE
(1761–1807) English
Self-portrait
Oil on canvas: 70 x 59.5 (oval)
Bequest of Patrick Shaw 1903
NG 911

Sir William Quiller ORCHARDSON
(1832–1910) Scottish
The Queen of the Swords
Oil on canvas: 48.8 x 81.9
Signed
Purchased 1910
NG 1018

Sir William Quiller ORCHARDSON
(1832–1910) Scottish
Master Baby
Oil on canvas: 109 x 168
Signed with initials and dated 1886
Purchased with the aid of an anonymous donor
1913
NG 1138

Sir William Quiller ORCHARDSON
(1832–1910) Scottish
*The Artist's Wife (Ellen Moxon,
Lady Orchardson, c. 1854–1917)*
Oil on canvas: 191 x 119.5
Signed and dated 1872
Bequest of Lady Orchardson 1917
NG 1207

Sir William Quiller ORCHARDSON
(1832–1910) Scottish
Miss Joanna Isabella Dick
Oil on canvas: 29.5 x 25.5
Presented by Allan Brugh Dick 1919
NG 1229

Sir William Quiller ORCHARDSON
(1832–1910) Scottish
Voltaire (1694–1778)
Oil on canvas: 201.7 x 147.2
Signed and dated 1883
Presented anonymously 1925
NG 1658

Sir William Quiller ORCHARDSON
(1832–1910) Scottish
The Rivals
Oil on canvas: 84 x 117
Signed with initials and dated 1895
Presented by Elspeth Tullis, Lady Invernairn
of Strathnairn; received after her death 1956
NG 2184

Sir William Quiller ORCHARDSON
(1832–1910) Scottish
*The Artist's Wife (Ellen Moxon, later Lady
Orchardson, c. 1854–1917)*
Oil on canvas: 29.5 x 29.5
Bequest of Sir James Lewis Caw 1951
NG 2215

Sir William Quiller ORCHARDSON
(1832–1910) Scottish
Through the Corn
Oil on canvas: 56.5 x 44.5
Reverse: with inscription
Purchased with the aid of the Barrogill Keith
Bequest Fund 1984
NG 2422

Bernard van ORLEY
(*c.* 1488–1541) Netherlandish
Before the Crucifixion
Oil on panel: 67.3 x 85.7
Purchased 1909
NG 995

Bernard van ORLEY
(*c. 1488–1541*) Netherlandish
Marie Haneton (died 1522)
Oil on panel: 75.2 x 56.2
Reverse: inscribed
Bequest of Sir Hugh Hume Campbell 1894
NG 1895

Attributed to Adriaen van OSTADE
(1610–85) Dutch
An Interior with a Pig's Carcase
Oil on panel: 46.3 x 57.8
Signed
Presented by W. Shiels to the RSA 1851;
transferred and presented 1910
NG 54

Isack van OSTADE
(1621–49) Dutch
Sportsmen Halting at an Inn
Oil on panel: 53.4 x 60.4
Signed and dated 1646
Bequest of Henry Callcott Brunning 1908
NG 951

Attributed to Samuel OWEN
(1768–1857) English
Homeward Bound
Oil on canvas: 100.3 x 80
Bequest of Gerard Hay Craig Sellar 1930;
received 1954
NG 1743

Giovanni Battista PAGGI
(1554–1627) Italian
The Rest on the Flight into Egypt
Oil on canvas: 86.5 x 68
Signed
Purchased by the RI 1830; transferred 1859
NG 55

Jean-Baptiste PATER
(1695–1736) French
Ladies Bathing
Oil on canvas: 58.6 x 71
Bequest of Lady Murray of Henderland 1861
NG 441

James PATERSON
(1854–1932) Scottish
Edinburgh from Craigleith
Oil on canvas: 67.4 x 114.3
Inscribed and signed
Purchased 1944
NG 2023

James PATERSON
(1854–1932) Scottish
The Estuary
Oil on paper laid on millboard: 17.7 x 25.3
Signed
Bequest of Dr Robert A. Lillie 1977
NG 2357

James PATERSON
(1854–1932) Scottish
Autumn in Glencairn, Moniaive
Oil on canvas: 102 x 127
Inscribed, signed and dated 1887
Purchased with the aid of the Barrogill Keith
Bequest Fund 1984
NG 2424

Sir Joseph Noel PATON
(1821–1901) Scottish
The Quarrel of Oberon and Titania
Oil on canvas: 99 x 152
Purchased by RAPFAS 1850; transferred 1897
NG 293

Sir Joseph Noel PATON
(1821–1901) Scottish
The Reconciliation of Oberon and Titania
Oil on canvas: 76.2 x 122.6
Signed and dated 1847
Purchased by the RSA 1848;
transferred and presented 1910
NG 294

Sir Joseph Noel PATON
(1821–1901) Scottish
Dawn: Luther at Erfurt
Oil on canvas: 92.7 x 69
Inscribed, signed in monogram and dated 1861
Purchased 1919
NG 1230

H. PEATTIE
(19th century) Scottish
Deanhaugh House
Oil on canvas: 38 x 51
Bequest of Miss Alice Leslie Inglis 1934
NG 2650

Attributed to Gonzalo PÉREZ
(15th century) Spanish
St Michael Vanquishing the Devil
Tempera and gold on panel: 191.8 x 104.5
Purchased 1910
NG 1021

Arthur PERIGAL
(1816–84) Scottish
Strowan Bridge
Oil on canvas: 52 x 74.3
Signed and dated 1856
Purchased 1937
NG 1874

Pietro PERUGINO (Vannucci)
(c. 1445/46–1523) Italian
Four Male Figures
Canvas: 73.3 x 55.5 (fragment)
Presented by the National Art Collections
Fund 1934
NG 1805

Imitator of Francesco PESELLINO
(c. 1422–57) Italian
*The Virgin and Child with the Infant St John
the Baptist*
Panel: 70.6 x 41.7
Purchased 1919
NG 1250

John PETTIE
(1839–93) Scottish
Who Goes ?
Oil on canvas: 77.5 x 57
Signed
Purchased 1913
NG 1131

John PETTIE
(1839–93) Scottish
Cromwell's Saints
Oil on canvas: 42.5 x 52
Signed and dated 1862
Bequest of John Jordan 1914
NG 1187

John PETTIE
(1839–93) Scottish
The Gambler's Victim
Oil on canvas: 67.5 x 97
Signed and dated 1869
Purchased 1982
NG 2414

John PETTIE
(1839–93) Scottish
William Waddell
Oil on canvas: 36.2 x 43.7
Signed and dated 1883
Bequest of Alan F. Stark 1983
NG 2417

John PHILLIP
(1817–67) Scottish
Spanish Boys Playing at Bull-fighting
Oil on canvas with chalk underdrawing: 136 x 214
(unfinished)
Purchased by RAPFAS 1867; transferred 1897
NG 534

John PHILLIP
(1817–67) Scottish
Ellen Brown, Mrs William Borthwick Johnstone
Oil on canvas: 49.8 x 60.3
Signed in monogram and dated 1861
Presented by the sitter 1868
NG 566

John PHILLIP
(1817–67) Scottish
'La Gloria': A Spanish Wake
Oil on canvas: 145.4 x 219.2
Signed in monogram and dated 1864
Purchased with a contribution
from John Ritchie Findlay 1897
NG 836

John PHILLIP
(1817–67) Scottish
William Borthwick Johnstone (1804–68)
Oil on canvas: 75 x 62.2
Signed in monogram and dated 1865
Presented by the artist to the RSA;
transferred and presented 1910
NG 1004

John PHILLIP
(1817–67) Scottish
Presbyterian Catechising
Oil on canvas: 100.6 x 156
Signed and dated 1847
Bequest of John Jordan 1914
NG 1155

John PHILLIP
(1817–67) Scottish
Self-portrait
Oil on canvas: 61.8 x 50.8
Bequest of James Mackinlay 1926
NG 1663

John PHILLIP
(1817–67) Scottish
Mary MacKay Caird, later Mrs James Glen (1847–1940)
Oil on canvas: 105.4 x 80
Signed in monogram and dated 1866
Bequest of Miss Elizabeth T. C. Glen 1945
NG 2028

John PHILLIP
(1817–67) Scottish
Two Boys: Study for 'Spanish Boys Playing at Bull-fighting' (NG 534)
Oil on canvas: 30.5 x 43.2
Reverse: with inscription
Purchased 1993
NG 2581

Henry William PICKERSGILL
(1782–1875) English
Portrait of a Gentleman
Oil on canvas: 63.5 x 55.7
Presented by G. Woodburn to the Board
of Manufactures *c.* 1852; transferred by 1882
NG 675

Style of PIERO di Cosimo
(c. 1462– after 1515) Italian
Two Censing Angels Holding a Crown
Panel: 93.3 x 183.5 (arched)
Bequest of Sir Claude Phillips 1924
NG 1633

Attributed to PIETRO da Cortona (Pietro
Berrettini)
(1596–1669) Italian
Landscape with St Mary Magdalene
Oil on canvas: 49 x 64.5
Purchased 1979
NG 2378

Circle of PIETRO da Cortona (Pietro Berrettini)
(1596–1669) Italian
Portrait of a Prelate
Oil on canvas: 124 x 95.5
Presented to the RI by Robert Clouston 1850;
transferred 1859
NG 109

Camille PISSARRO
(1830–1903) French
The Marne at Chennevières
Oil on canvas: 91.5 x 145.5
Signed
Purchased 1947
NG 2098

Camille PISSARRO
(1830–1903) French
Kitchen Gardens at L'Hermitage, Pontoise
Oil on canvas: 54 x 65.1
Signed and dated 1874
Presented by Mrs Isabel M. Traill 1979
NG 2384

Giovanni Battista PITTONI
(1687–1767) Italian
The Apotheosis of St Jerome with St Peter
of Alcántara and an Unidentified Franciscan
Oil on canvas: 275 x 143
Purchased 1960
NG 2238

POLIDORO da Lanciano (Polidoro di Paolo
di Renzi)
(*c.* 1515–65) Italian
The Holy Family
Oil on panel: 42.6 x 52
Purchased by the RI 1852; transferred 1859
NG 105

POLIDORO da Lanciano (Polidoro di Paolo
di Renzi)
(*c.* 1515–65) Italian
The Virgin and Sleeping Child
Oil on canvas: 53 x 67.3
Bequest of the 11th Marquess of Lothian 1941
NG 1931

POPPI (Francesco Morandini)
(1544–97) Italian
The Golden Age
Oil on panel: 43 x 32.6
Purchased 1964
NG 2268

Frans POURBUS the Elder
(1545–81) Netherlandish
George, 5th Lord Seton (c. 1531–85)
and his Family
Oil on panel: 109 x 79
Inscribed, signed with initials and dated 1572
Bequest of Sir Theophilus Biddulph 1948;
received 1965
NG 2275

Pieter POURBUS
(1523/24–1584) Netherlandish
A Married Lady of Bruges, aged 26
Oil on panel: 49.4 x 39.9
Inscribed, signed with initials and dated 1565
Purchased 1909
NG 991

Nicolas POUSSIN
(1594–1665) French
The Mystic Marriage of St Catherine
Oil on panel: 126 x 168
Bequest of Sir John Heathcoat Amory 1973
NG 2319

Nicolas POUSSIN
(1594–1665) French
Moses Striking the Rock
Oil on canvas: 98.5 x 136
Lent by the Duke of Sutherland 1945

Nicolas POUSSIN
(1594–1665) French
The Sacrament of Baptism
Oil on canvas: 117 x 178
Lent by the Duke of Sutherland 1945

Nicolas POUSSIN
(1594–1665) French
The Sacrament of Confirmation
Oil on canvas: 117 x 178
Lent by the Duke of Sutherland 1945

Nicolas POUSSIN
(1594–1665) French
The Sacrament of Marriage
Oil on canvas: 117 x 178
Lent by the Duke of Sutherland 1945

Nicolas POUSSIN
(1594–1665) French
The Sacrament of Penance
Oil on canvas: 117 x 178
Lent by the Duke of Sutherland 1945

Nicolas POUSSIN
(1594–1665) French
The Sacrament of Ordination
Oil on canvas: 117 x 178
Lent by the Duke of Sutherland 1945

Nicolas POUSSIN
(1594–1665) French
The Sacrament of the Holy Eucharist
Oil on canvas: 117 x 178
Lent by the Duke of Sutherland 1945

Nicolas POUSSIN
(1594–1665) French
The Sacrament of Extreme Unction
Oil on canvas: 117 x 178
Lent by the Duke of Sutherland 1945

John POWELL
(active 1780 – after 1833) English
Stephen Henry Hough (1776– after 1828)
Oil on canvas: 63.8 x 45.7
Presented by J. A. F. Hamilton 1967
NG 2298

Giulio Cesare PROCACCINI
(1574–1625) Italian
Cupid
Oil on canvas: 70 x 95.5 (fragment)
Purchased by the RI 1830; transferred 1859
NG 63

Giulio Cesare PROCACCINI
(1574–1625) Italian
The Raising of the Cross
Oil on canvas: 218 x 148.6
Purchased 1965
NG 2276

Giulio Cesare PROCACCINI
(1574–1625) Italian
*The Virgin and Child with the Infant St John the
Baptist and Attendant Angels*
Oil on panel: 51 x 36.5
Purchased with the aid of the Heritage Lottery
Fund and the National Art Collections Fund 1995
NG 2647

Jan PROVOST
(active 1494 – died 1529) Netherlandish
The Virgin and Child
Oil on panel: 35.6 x 21.3 (arched)
Purchased 1921
NG 1537

Pierre PUVIS DE CHAVANNES
(1824–98) French
Vigilance
Oil on canvas: 106 x 53.2
Signed and dated 1867
Purchased 1929
NG 1739

Attributed to François QUESNEL
(1543–1619) French
*Renault de Beaune, Archbishop
of Bourges (1527–1609)*
Oil on panel: 36.2 x 26
With inscription
Presented by the National Art Collections Fund
from the Alexander Bequest 1972
NG 2317

Sir Henry RAEBURN
(1756–1823) Scottish
*Margarita MacDonald, Mrs Robert Scott
Moncrieff (died 1824)*
Oil on canvas: 76.5 x 64
Bequest of Robert Scott Moncrieff to the RSA 1854;
transferred and presented 1910
NG 302

Sir Henry RAEBURN
(1756–1823) Scottish
*Colonel Alastair Ranaldson Macdonell
of Glengarry (1771–1828)*
Oil on canvas: 241.9 x 151.1
Purchased 1917
NG 420

Sir Henry RAEBURN
(1756–1823) Scottish
Sir Charles Hay, Lord Newton (1740–1811)
Oil on canvas: 74.3 x 61
Bequest of Mrs Malcolm Laing 1864
NG 522

Sir Henry RAEBURN
(1756–1823) Scottish
*Frances Harriet Wynne, Mrs Hamilton
of Kames (1786–1860)*
Oil on canvas: 236 x 148.6
Presented by Sir William Stirling-Maxwell 1877
NG 623

Sir Henry RAEBURN
(1756–1823) Scottish
Jean or Jane Adam, Mrs Kennedy of Dunure
Oil on canvas: 125 x 100.3
Presented by John Heugh to the RSA 1877;
transferred and presented 1910
NG 626

Sir Henry RAEBURN
(1756–1823) Scottish
John Wauchope (1751–1828)
Oil on canvas: 76.5 x 64.2
Presented by the Revd H. B. Sands 1884
NG 681

Sir Henry RAEBURN
(1756–1823) Scottish
Charlotte Hall, Lady Hume Campbell of
Marchmont, and her son, Sir Hugh Hume
Campbell, 7th Bart of Marchmont (1812–1901)
Oil on canvas: 197 x 151
Bequest of Sir Hugh Hume Campbell 1894
NG 831

Sir Henry RAEBURN
(1756–1823) Scottish
Christina Lamont Drummond, Mrs Dougald
Campbell of Ballimore (1735–1810)
Oil on canvas: 122.6 x 97.8
Bequest of Lady Riddell 1897
NG 837

Sir Henry RAEBURN
(1756–1823) Scottish
Alexander Bonar of Ratho (1750–1820)
Oil on canvas: 76.2 x 63.5 (cut down)
Presented by Miss S. A. Fleming 1900
NG 845

Sir Henry RAEBURN
(1756–1823) Scottish
Sarah McCall, Mrs Alexander Bonar
Oil on canvas: 76.2 x 63.5 (cut down)
Presented by Miss S. A. Fleming 1900
NG 846

Sir Henry RAEBURN
(1756–1823) Scottish
Major William Clunes (fl. 1790–1812)
Oil on canvas: 236 x 150
Bequest of Lady Siemens to the RSA 1902;
transferred and presented 1910
NG 903

Sir Henry RAEBURN
(1756–1823) Scottish
Self-portrait
Oil on canvas: 89 x 69.5
Purchased 1905
NG 930

Sir Henry RAEBURN
(1756–1823) Scottish
John Smith of Craigend (1739–1816)
Oil on canvas: 75 x 63.5
Purchased 1911
NG 1027

Sir Henry RAEBURN
(1756–1823) Scottish
Justina Camilla Wynne, Mrs Alexander Finlay
of Glencorse (1785–1814)
Oil on canvas: 226 x 151.2
Bequest of Mrs Glassford Bell 1915;
transferred from the SNPG
NG 1192

Sir Henry RAEBURN
(1756–1823) Scottish
William Beveridge
Oil on canvas: 92.3 x 70
Bequest of Mrs Lake Gloag 1917
NG 1199

Sir Henry RAEBURN
(1756–1823) Scottish
George Kinnear (1751–1823)
Oil on canvas: 87.6 x 68
Bequest of Miss Kinnear 1919
NG 1222

Sir Henry RAEBURN
(1756–1823) Scottish
*Fearne Gardiner, Mrs George Kinnear
(1771–1846)*
Oil on canvas: 89.5 x 69.5
Bequest of Miss Kinnear 1919
NG 1223

Sir Henry RAEBURN
(1756–1823) Scottish
Lieutenant-Colonel George Lyon (fl. 1788–1801)
Oil on canvas: 90.6 x 70.6
Bequest of Miss Kinnear 1919
NG 1224

Sir Henry RAEBURN
(1756–1823) Scottish
Dr Gardiner (1726–1807)
Oil on canvas: 89 x 67.5
Bequest of Miss Kinnear 1919
NG 1225

Sir Henry RAEBURN
(1756–1823) Scottish
A Dog
Oil on canvas: 69.8 x 90.2
Purchased 1919
NG 1236

Sir Henry RAEBURN
(1756–1823) Scottish
David Deuchar (1743–1808)
Watercolour on ivory: 6.1 x 4.8 (oval)
Reverse: with inscription
Purchased with a contribution from
Melville Gray 1931
NG 1762

Sir Henry RAEBURN
(1756–1823) Scottish
A Lady in a Lace Cap
Oil on canvas: 92 x 71
Bequest of Miss Alice Leslie Inglis 1934
NG 1816

Sir Henry RAEBURN
(1756–1823) Scottish
Miss Lamont of Greenock
Oil on canvas: 75.8 x 63
Bequest of Mrs Agnes Duncan Miller in memory
of her husband Robert Miller 1937
NG 1878

Sir Henry RAEBURN
(1756–1823) Scottish
James Thomson of Nether Bogie (1749–1831)
Oil on canvas: 127.7 x 101
Presented by Mrs Florence Davidson 1940
NG 1923

Sir Henry RAEBURN
(1756–1823) Scottish
Zepherina Loughnan, Mrs Henry Veitch of Eliock
Oil on canvas: 123 x 98.4
Presented by Francis Neilson through the
National Art Collections Fund in memory
of his mother 1946
NG 2034

Sir Henry RAEBURN
(1756–1823) Scottish
Portrait of a Jew
Oil on canvas: 76.2 x 63.5
Presented by Mrs F. C. Holland 1948
NG 2108

Sir Henry RAEBURN
(1756–1823) Scottish
Revd Dr Robert Walker (1755–1808) Skating
on Duddingston Loch
Oil on canvas: 76.2 x 63.5
Purchased 1949
NG 2112

Sir Henry RAEBURN
(1756–1823) Scottish
Sir Patrick Inglis, 5th Bart
of Cramond (died 1817)
Oil on canvas: 125.7 x 100.3
With inscription
Bequest of Sir John Douglas Don-Wauchope 1951
NG 2147

Sir Henry RAEBURN
(1756–1823) Scottish
James Wauchope of Edmonstone (1767–97)
Oil on canvas: 90.2 x 69.3
With inscription
Bequest of Sir John Douglas Don-Wauchope 1951
NG 2148

Sir Henry RAEBURN
(1756–1823) Scottish
John Wauchope of Edmonstone (1742–1810)
Oil on canvas: 75.6 x 62.9
With inscription
Bequest of Sir John Douglas Don-Wauchope 1951
NG 2149

Sir Henry RAEBURN
(1756–1823) Scottish
Anne Erskine, Mrs John Wauchope
of Edmonstone (1740–1811)
Oil on canvas: 75.6 x 62.9
With inscription
Bequest of Sir John Douglas Don-Wauchope 1951
NG 2150

Sir Henry RAEBURN
(1756–1823) Scottish
Thomas Francis Kennedy of Dunure (1788–1879)
Oil on canvas: 127.3 x 101.9
Presented by Elspeth Tullis, Lady Invernairn of
Strathnairn; received after her death 1956
NG 2181

Sir Henry RAEBURN
(1756–1823) Scottish
Jean or Jane Adam, Mrs Kennedy of Dunure
Oil on canvas: 127 x 101.9
Presented by Elspeth Tullis, Lady Invernairn
of Strathnairn; received after her death 1956
NG 2182

Sir Henry RAEBURN
(1756–1823) Scottish
Elizabeth Forbes, Mrs Colin Mackenzie
of Portmore (died 1840)
Oil on canvas: 126.5 x 100.4
Bequest of Lieutenant-Colonel J. C. Dundas 1967
NG 2296

Sir Henry RAEBURN
(1756–1823) Scottish
Sir John Sinclair, 1st Bart of Ulbster (1734–1835)
Oil on canvas: 238.5 x 152.5
With inscription
Purchased with the aid of a Treasury Grant 1967
NG 2301

Sir Henry RAEBURN
(1756–1823) Scottish
David Hunter of Blackness (died 1809)
Oil on canvas: 76 x 61.5
Bequest of Mrs Elizabeth Adeline Powell 1977
NG 2394

After Sir Henry RAEBURN
(1756–1823) Scottish
Henry Raeburn (1784–1863) on a Grey Pony
Oil on canvas laid on panel: 35.3 x 23.5
Purchased 1911
NG 1026

Allan RAMSAY
(1713–84) Scottish
The Artist's Wife (Margaret Lindsay of Evelick,
c. 1726–82)
Oil on canvas: 74.3 x 61.9
Bequest of Lady Murray of Henderland 1861
NG 430

Allan RAMSAY
(1713–84) Scottish
Jean-Jacques Rousseau (1712–78)
Oil on canvas: 74.9 x 64.8
Purchased 1890
NG 820

Allan RAMSAY
(1713–84) Scottish
Mrs Anna Bruce of Arnot (died 1810)
Oil on canvas: 74.8 x 62
Signed and with inscription (no longer visible)
Purchased 1907
NG 946

Allan RAMSAY
(1713–84) Scottish
Mary Digges, Lady Robert Manners (1737–1829)
Oil on canvas: 76 x 63.5 (oval)
Bequest of Mrs Nisbet Hamilton Ogilvy
of Biel 1921
NG 1523

Allan RAMSAY
(1713–84) Scottish
Lady Lucy Manners, Duchess of Montrose
(1717–88)
Oil on canvas: 74 x 61.6
Signed and dated 1739
Bequest of Mrs Nisbet Hamilton Ogilvy
of Biel 1921
NG 1524

Allan RAMSAY
(1713–84) Scottish
Portrait of a Lady, formerly called Flora Macdonald
Oil on canvas: 74.9 x 62.2
Signed and dated 1752
Bequest of Mrs Morag Macdonald 1937
NG 1884

Allan RAMSAY
(1713–84) Scottish
James Ker of Bughtrigg (1700–68)
Oil on canvas: 74.9 x 62.2
Signed and dated 1754
Presented by Mrs F. G. Kerr 1937
NG 1889

Allan RAMSAY
(1713–84) Scottish
Sir Peter Halkett Wedderburn, 1st Bart of Pitfirrane and Gosford (c. 1659–1746)
Oil on canvas: 76.3 x 63.3
Inscribed, signed and dated 1746
Bequest of C. J. G. Paterson 1942
NG 1960

Allan RAMSAY
(1713–84) Scottish
George Bristow (1727–1815)
Oil on canvas: 127 x 101.6
Signed and dated 1750
Purchased 1949
NG 2119

Allan RAMSAY
(1713–84) Scottish
Elizabeth, Mrs Daniel Cunyngham
Oil on canvas: 238 x 146
Purchased 1951
NG 2133

Allan RAMSAY
(1713–84) Scottish
Sir John Inglis, 2nd Bart of Cramond (1683–1771)
Oil on canvas: 76.2 x 63.5
With inscription
Bequest of Sir John Douglas Don-Wauchope 1951
NG 2151

Allan RAMSAY
(1713–84) Scottish
Anne Cockburn, Lady Inglis (died 1772)
Oil on canvas: 76.2 x 63.5
With inscription
Bequest of Sir John Douglas Don-Wauchope 1951
NG 2152

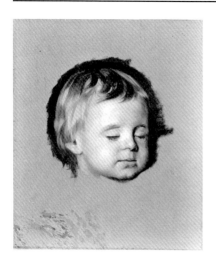

Allan RAMSAY
(1713–84) Scottish
A Study of a Dead Child
Oil on canvas: 32 x 27.3
Presented by Lady Murray of Henderland
as a memorial to her husband, Lord Murray
of Henderland 1860
NG 2295

Allan RAMSAY
(1713–84) Scottish
Thomas Lamb of Rye (1719–1804)
Oil on canvas: 103.5 x 87.8
Signed and dated 1753
Accepted in lieu of tax 1992
NG 2545

Formerly attributed to Allan RAMSAY
(1713–84) Scottish
*Caroline D'Arcy, 4th Marchioness of Lothian
(died 1778)*
Oil on canvas: 238 x 147
Bequest of the 11th Marquess of Lothian 1941
NG 1935

RAPHAEL (Raffaello Santi)
(1483–1520) Italian
The Holy Family with a Palm Tree
Oil and gold on canvas, transferred from panel:
101.5 (circular)
Lent by the Duke of Sutherland 1945

RAPHAEL (Raffaello Santi)
(1483–1520) Italian
*The Virgin and Child
('The Bridgewater Madonna')*
Oil and gold on canvas, transferred from panel:
82 x 57
Lent by the Duke of Sutherland 1945

RAPHAEL (Raffaello Santi) and Studio
(1483–1520) Italian
*The Holy Family Meeting the Infant St John the
Baptist ('The Madonna del Passeggio')*
Oil on panel: 90 x 63.3
Reverse: with inscription
Lent by the Duke of Sutherland 1945

After RAPHAEL (Raffaello Santi)
(1483–1520) Italian
St Peter
Oil on canvas: 83.7 x 67.7
Acquired by the RI 1830; transferred 1859
NG 110

After RAPHAEL (Raffaello Santi)
(1483–1520) Italian
*The Virgin and Child with the Infant St John the
Baptist ('The Aldobrandini or Garvagh Madonna')*
Oil and gold on panel: 29.5 x 22.3
Presented by Mr and Mrs J. Percy Callard 1936
NG 1854

After RAPHAEL (Raffaello Santi)
(1483–1520) Italian
The Madonna with the Veil ('La Vierge au diadème bleu')
Oil on panel: 68.5 x 47.8
Lent by the Duke of Sutherland 1945

Sir George REID
(1841–1913) Scottish
Norham Castle
Oil on canvas: 59.7 x 90.2
Signed in monogram and dated 1879
Purchased 1929
NG 1740

REMBRANDT (Rembrandt van Rijn)
(1606–69) Dutch
A Woman in Bed
Oil on canvas: 81.1 x 67.8 (arched)
Signed and dated 164[ ]
Presented by William McEwan 1885
NG 827

REMBRANDT (Rembrandt van Rijn)
(1606–69) Dutch
Self-portrait, aged 51
Oil on canvas: 53 x 44
Signed and dated 1657
Lent by the Duke of Sutherland 1945

Studio of REMBRANDT (Rembrandt van Rijn)
(1606–69) Dutch
A Young Woman with Flowers in her Hair
Oil on panel: 70.9 x 53.1 (oval)
Signed and dated 1634
Lent by the Duke of Sutherland 1945

Studio of REMBRANDT (Rembrandt van Rijn)
(1606–69) Dutch
Hannah and Samuel
Oil on panel: 42.9 x 34.8
Signed and dated 1650
Lent by the Duke of Sutherland 1945

Follower of REMBRANDT (Rembrandt van Rijn)
(1606–69) Dutch
A Study of a Man's Head ('Portrait of a Jew')
Oil on panel: 21 x 17.8
Lent by the Duke of Sutherland 1945

Guido RENI
(1575–164?) Italian
Moses with Pharoah's Crown
Oil on canvas: 132.2 x 172.7
Purchased 1979
NG 2375

Auguste RENOIR
(1841–1919) French
A Woman Nursing a Child
Oil on canvas: 41.2 x 32.5
Signed
Presented by Sir Alexander Maitland in memory
of his wife Rosalind 1960
NG 2230

Pandolfo RESCHI
(c. 1640–96) Italian
A Battle
Oil on canvas: 95 x 147.3
Purchased by the RI 1831; transferred 1859
NG 70

Sir Joshua REYNOLDS
(1723–92) English
James Coutts (1733–78)
Oil on panel: 52.7 x 43.2
Reverse: inscribed
Presented by Lord Elcho 1859
NG 338

Sir Joshua REYNOLDS
(1723–92) English
*Sir David Lindsay, 4th Bart
of Evelick* (c. 1732–97)
Oil on canvas: 76.2 x 63.4
Bequest of Lady Murray of Henderland 1861
NG 427

Sir Joshua REYNOLDS
(1723–92) English
Captain Adam Duncan, later Admiral Duncan and
1st Viscount of Camperdown (1731–1804)
Oil on canvas: 127 x 101
Bequest of the Earl of Camperdown 1918
NG 1215

Sir Joshua REYNOLDS
(1723–92) English
A Little Girl (possibly Lady Frances Scott,
later Lady Douglas, 1750–1817)
Oil on canvas: 76 x 63
Purchased 1926
NG 1666

Sir Joshua REYNOLDS
(1723–92) English
The Ladies Waldegrave: Lady Charlotte Maria
Waldegrave, later Countess of Euston and
Duchess of Grafton (1761–1808); Lady Elizabeth
Laura Waldegrave, later Countess Waldegrave
(1760–1816); and Lady Anna Horatia
Waldegrave, later Lady Seymour (1762–1801)
Oil on canvas: 143 x 168.3
Purchased with the aid of the National Art
Collections Fund 1952
NG 2171

Sir Joshua REYNOLDS
(1723–92) English
Alexander Douglas-Hamilton,
later 10th Duke of Hamilton and 7th Duke
of Brandon (1767–1852)
Oil on canvas: 67.5 x 53.5
Presented by Elspeth Tullis, Lady Invernairn
of Strathnairn; received after her death 1956
NG 2183

Studio of Jusepe de RIBERA
(1591–1652) Spanish
A Philosopher ('A Mathematician')
Oil on canvas: 116.9 x 91.5
Acquired by the RSA by 1859; transferred and
presented 1910
NG 83

Follower of Jusepe de RIBERA
(1591–1652) Spanish
The Martyrdom of St Sebastian
Oil on canvas: 202 x 146.5
Presented to the RI by Charles O'Neil 1834;
transferred 1859
NG 84

Attributed to Marco RICCI (1676–1729) and
Sebastiano RICCI (1659–1734)
Italian
Landscape with Monks
Oil on canvas: 95 x 127.5
Purchased by the RI 1831; transferred 1859
NG 7

Sebastiano RICCI
(1659–1734) Italian
Christ Healing the Blind Man
Oil on canvas: 52 x 67.5
Purchased with the aid of the National Art
Collections Fund 1994
NG 2623

David ROBERTS
(1796–1864) Scottish
*Rome: Sunset from the Convent of Sant' Onofrio
on the Janiculum*
Oil on canvas: 213 x 427
Signed and dated 1856
Presented by the artist to the RSA 1857;
transferred and presented 1910
NG 304

David ROBERTS
(1796–1864) Scottish
A Study for 'Rome: Sunset from the Convent
of Sant' Onofrio on the Janiculum' (NG 304)
Oil on panel: 21.6 x 41
Purchased 1963
NG 2261

Alexander Ignatius ROCHE
(1861–1921) Scottish
Nell
Oil on canvas: 50.7 x 43.9
Signed
Bequest of Alexander F. Roberts 1929
NG 1733

Alexander Ignatius ROCHE
(1861–1921) Scottish
Afternoon Sunshine, St Monans
Oil on panel: 26.7 x 35
Signed
Bequest of Sir James Lewis Caw 1951
NG 2143

Alexander Ignatius ROCHE
(1861–1921) Scottish
Roses
Oil on panel: 27 x 30
Signed
Bequest of Dr Robert A. Lillie 1977
NG 2360

Alexander Ignatius ROCHE
(1861–1921) Scottish
The Old Fisherman
Oil on canvas: 46 x 61
Signed
Bequest of Mr and Mrs G. D. Robinson through
the National Art Collections Fund 1988
NG 2457

Attributed to Pieter ROESTRAETEN
(*c.* 1631–1700) Dutch
Still Life with Musical Instruments
Reverse: *A Man's Head* (unfinished, see
next item)
Oil on copper: 39.3 x 58
Signed in monogram
Bequest of the 11th Marquess of Lothian 1941
NG 1937

Attributed to Pieter ROESTRAETEN
(c. 1631–1700) Dutch
A Man's Head (unfinished) with inscription
Reverse of NG 1937

ROMAN School
(17th century)
Cain Killing Abel
Oil on canvas: 190 x 143
Presented to the RI by Sir Alexander Crichton
1833; transferred 1859
NG 21

George ROMNEY
(1734–1802) English
Mary Bootle, Mrs Wilbraham Bootle (died 1813)
Oil on canvas: 123.9 x 99.7
Purchased with the aid of the Cowan Smith
Bequest Fund 1927
NG 1674

After Salvator ROSA
(1615–73) Italian
A Figure in Armour
Oil on canvas: 87 x 60.2
Bequest of Lady Belhaven 1873
NG 600

After Salvator ROSA
(1615–73) Italian
A Figure in Armour
Oil on canvas: 87.5 x 60.5
Bequest of Lady Belhaven 1873
NG 600 A

After Salvator ROSA
(1615–73) Italian
A River Scene with Figures
Oil on canvas: 36.2 x 89.2
Bequest of Mrs Mary Veitch to the RSA 1875;
transferred and presented 1910
NG 622

Joseph Thorburn ROSS
(1849–1903) Scottish
The Bass Rock
Oil on canvas: 147.8 x 147.8
Signed
Presented by friends and admirers
of the artist 1904
NG 920

Robert Thorburn ROSS
(1816–76) Scottish
Sunshine
Oil on canvas: 85.5 x 111
Signed and dated 1871
Bequest of John Scott 1864;
received through Mrs Elizabeth Scott 1878
NG 632

Cosimo ROSSELLI
(1439–1507) Italian
*St Catherine of Siena as Spiritual Mother
of the Second and Third Orders of St Dominic*
Tempera and gold on panel: 170 x 171.5
Purchased 1911
NG 1030

Dante Gabriel Charles ROSSETTI
(1828–82) English
Beata Beatrix
Oil on canvas: 86 x 66.7
Signed and dated 1880
Presented by A. E. Anderson in memory
of his brother Frank 1928
NG 1721

Sir Peter Paul RUBENS
(1577–1640) Flemish
A Study of a Head (St Ambrose)
Oil on panel: 49.6 x 38.1
Purchased with the aid of the Cowan Smith
Bequest Fund 1947
NG 2097

Sir Peter Paul RUBENS
(1577–1640) Flemish
The Feast of Herod
Oil on canvas: 208 x 264
Purchased 1958
NG 2193

Sir Peter Paul RUBENS
(1577–1640) Flemish
The Adoration of the Shepherds
Oil on panel: 73.8 x 92.4
Purchased 1970
NG 2311

Sir Peter Paul RUBENS
(1577–1640) Flemish
The Reconciliation of Esau and Jacob
Oil on panel: 42.5 x 40.3
Accepted in lieu of tax 1980
NG 2397

Jacob van RUISDAEL
(c. 1628–82) Dutch
The Banks of a River
Oil on canvas: 134 x 193
Signed and dated 1649
Sir James Erskine of Torrie Bequest
to the University of Edinburgh, deposited
on loan 1845 with the RI; loan transferred
to the National Gallery of Scotland 1859

Alexander RUNCIMAN
(1736–85) Scottish
Italian River Landscape with a Hermit
Oil on panel: 28.6 x 36.8
Signed in monogram
Purchased 1887
NG 790

Alexander RUNCIMAN
(1736–85) Scottish
Hubert and Arthur (from Shakespeare's 'King John')
Oil on canvas: 57 x 78.5
Signed and dated 1780
Presented by Sir Alec and Lady Martin through the National Art Collections Fund 1957
NG 2189

Alexander RUNCIMAN
(1736–85) Scottish
The Death of Dido
Oil on canvas: 102 x 131.2
Signed and dated 1778
Accepted in lieu of tax 1992
NG 2543

Alexander RUNCIMAN
(1736–85) Scottish
Agrippina Landing at Brundisium with the Ashes of Germanicus
Oil on canvas: 100.2 x 133.2
Inscribed, signed and dated 1780
Reverse: inscribed
Accepted in lieu of tax 1992
NG 2544

John RUNCIMAN
(1744–68/69) Scottish
King Lear in the Storm
Oil on panel: 44.8 x 61
Signed and dated 1767
Reverse: with inscription
Bequest of David Laing 1879
NG 570

John RUNCIMAN
(1744–68/69) Scottish
The Flight into Egypt
Oil on panel: 29.9 x 22.3
Signed
Bequest of David Laing 1879
NG 648

John RUNCIMAN
(1744–68/69) Scottish
The Temptation of Our Lord
Oil on panel: 18.4 x 28.6
Purchased 1887
NG 792

John RUNCIMAN
(1744–68/69) Scottish
Christ with his Disciples on the Road to Emmaus
Oil on copper: 16.5 x 21.6
Signed with initials
Purchased 1887
NG 793

John RUNCIMAN
(1744–68/69) Scottish
Salome Receiving St John the Baptist's Head
Oil on panel: 18.4 x 13.3
Reverse: with inscription
Presented by William Nelson to the RSA 1887;
transferred and presented 1910
NG 1005

John RUNCIMAN
(1744–68/69) Scottish
The Good Samaritan
Oil on panel: 22.6 x 28.3 (irregular)
Purchased 1949
NG 2116

Pieter Jansz. SAENREDAM
(1597–1665) Dutch
*The Interior of St Bavo's Church, Haarlem
(the 'Grote Kerk')*
Oil on panel: 174.8 x 143.6
Inscribed, signed and dated 1648
Purchased by Private Treaty with the aid of the
National Heritage Memorial Fund, the National
Art Collections Fund (William Leng Bequest)
and the Pilgrim Trust 1982
NG 2413

Herman SAFTLEVEN
(1609–85) Dutch
Christ Preaching from a Boat
Oil on panel: 75 x 108
Signed in monogram and dated 1642
Bequest of Mrs Nisbet Hamilton Ogilvy
of Biel 1921
NG 1508

Workshop of SANO di Pietro (Ansano di Pietro
di Mencio)
(1406–81) Italian
The Coronation of the Virgin
Tempera and gold on panel: 72.7 x 43.5
Purchased 1922
NG 1565

Dirk SANTVOORT
(1610/11–1680) Dutch
'The Young Housekeeper'
Oil on panel: 122 x 92
Presented by William Wright 1881
NG 663

John Singer SARGENT
(1856–1925) American
Gertrude, Lady Agnew of Lochnaw (1865–1932)
Oil on canvas: 127 x 101
Signed
Purchased with the aid of the Cowan Smith
Bequest Fund 1925
NG 1656

John Singer SARGENT
(1856–1925) American
*Constance Wynne-Roberts, Mrs Ernest Hills
of Redleaf (died 1932)*
Oil on canvas: 156 x 102
Signed
Bequest of Mrs Ernest Hills 1933
NG 1787

Andrea del SARTO
(1486–1530) Italian
Domenico di Jacopo di Matteo Becuccio
Oil on panel: 86 x 67
Purchased 1967
NG 2297

Godfried SCHALCKEN
(1643–1706) Dutch
A Boy Blowing on a Firebrand to Light a Candle
Oil on canvas: 75 x 63.5
Purchased with the aid of the National Art
Collections Fund and the National Heritage
Memorial Fund 1989
NG 2495

John Christian SCHETKY
(1778–1874) Scottish
A Sea-piece
Oil on canvas: 90.5 x 127
Signed and dated 1843
Presented by the Misses Schetky 1886
NG 786

Sinibaldo SCORZA
(1589–1631) Italian
Landscape with Philemon and Baucis
Oil on canvas: 48 x 72
Purchased by the RI 1830; transferred 1859
NG 76

Sinibaldo SCORZA
(1589–1631) Italian
Landscape with Latona and the Peasants
Oil on canvas: 48 x 72
Purchased by the RI 1830; transferred 1859
NG 77

David SCOTT
(1806–49) Scottish
The Vintager
Oil on canvas: 116.9 x 97.2
Signed
Presented by Andrew Coventry 1859
NG 342

David SCOTT
(1806–49) Scottish
*Alchemystical Adept (Paracelsus) Lecturing
on the Elixir Vitae*
Oil on canvas: 149 x 186
Signed and dated 1838
Purchased by RAPFAS 1887; transferred 1897
NG 796

David SCOTT
(1806–49) Scottish
*Philoctetes left on the Isle of Lemnos by the Greeks
on their passage towards Troy*
Oil on canvas: 101 x 119.4
Presented by J. W. Cousin 1890
NG 825

David SCOTT
(1806–49) Scottish
The Traitor's Gate
Oil on panel: 137 x 183.4
Presented by Robert Carfrae 1899
NG 843

David SCOTT
(1806–49) Scottish
Puck Fleeing from the Dawn
Oil on canvas: 95.3 x 146
Signed and dated 1837
Purchased 1909
NG 992

David SCOTT
(1806–49) Scottish
Ariel and Caliban
Oil on canvas: 116.8 x 98.5
Signed and dated 1837
Purchased by the RSA 1849;
transferred and presented 1910
NG 1006

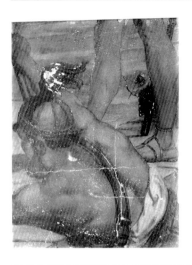

David SCOTT
(1806–49) Scottish
'The Fall of the Giants'
Fresco: 99 x 74.3 (fragment)
Bequest of Miss Fairbairn 1914
NG 1147

David SCOTT
(1806–49) Scottish
The Fire of London
Oil on canvas: 52 x 95.5
Presented by Arthur Kay 1924
NG 1647

David SCOTT
(1806–49) Scottish
A Study for 'The Descent from the Cross'
Oil on paper laid on canvas: 47 x 39.3
Reverse: inscribed, signed with initials
and dated 1837
Purchased 1927
NG 1676

David SCOTT
(1806–49) Scottish
*The Dead Sarpedon, Borne by Sleep and Death
(from Homer's 'The Iliad')*
Oil on canvas: 179 x 141
Reverse: signed
Presented by Miss Isabella Spring Brown 1930
NG 1751

David SCOTT
(1806–49) Scottish
The Pursuit of Fortune
Oil on canvas: 50.8 x 93.4
Signed
Bequest of Miss Isabella Spring Brown 1937
NG 1876

David SCOTT
(1806–49) Scottish
Dr Samuel Brown (1817–56)
Oil on canvas: 77.5 x 64.8
Bequest of Miss Isabella Spring Brown 1937
NG 1877

David SCOTT
(1806–49) Scottish
The Belated Peasant (from Milton's
'Paradise Lost')
Oil on canvas: 73.6 x 92.4
Signed
Purchased 1946
NG 2072

David SCOTT
(1806–49) Scottish
John Stirling (1811–82)
Oil on canvas: 76.2 x 63.5
Purchased 1946
NG 2073

David SCOTT
(1806–49) Scottish
William Bell Scott (1811–90)
Oil on canvas: 76 x 63
Inscribed
Presented by Miss Courtney-Boyd 1949
NG 2118

William Bell SCOTT
(1811–90) Scottish
Albrecht Dürer in Nürnberg
Oil on canvas: 60.4 x 73
Purchased 1909
NG 969

William Bell SCOTT
(1811–90) Scottish
*Una and the Lion (from Spenser's
'The Faerie Queene')*
Oil on canvas: 91.5 x 71.2
Purchased 1978
NG 2367

William Bell SCOTT
(1811–90) Scottish
Port na Curachan, Iona
Oil on canvas: 56 x 73.7
Inscribed, signed and dated 1887
Purchased 1978
NG 2368

William Bell SCOTT
(1811–90) Scottish
The Nativity
Oil on canvas: 74 x 114
Signed in monogram and dated 1872
Purchased 1980
NG 2396

SCOTTISH School
(18th century)
A View of Loch Katrine
Oil on canvas: 90 x 113
Purchased 1993
NG 2614

SCOTTISH School
(19th century)
*The Interior of the National Gallery of Scotland,
c. 1867–1877*
Oil on canvas: 50.5 x 61
Purchased 1967
NG 2299

Jacopo del SELLAIO (Jacopo di Arcangelo)
(*c.* 1441–93) Italian
*Christ as the Man of Sorrows, with the Archangel
Raphael, the Young Tobias and St Sebastian*
Panel: 28.8 x 43.4
Bequest of the 11th Marquess of Lothian 1941
NG 1941

Attributed to Jacopo del SELLAIO (Jacopo
di Arcangelo)
(*c.* 1441–93) Italian
*A Triumphal Procession: The Reception and
Coronation of a Prince or Victor*
Panel: 44 x 167.7
Purchased 1921
NG 1538

Adolf SENFF
(1785–1863) German
A Study of Plants
Oil on paper laid on cardboard: 28.6 x 42.4
Inscribed, signed and dated 1828
Purchased 1993
NG 2562

Giovanni SERODINE
(1600–30) Italian
The Tribute Money
Oil on canvas: 146 x 227
Bequest of Mrs Nisbet Hamilton Ogilvy
of Biel 1921
NG 1513

John Thomas SETON
(active 1761–1806) Scottish
William Fullerton of Carstairs (1720–1806),
and Captain Ninian Lowis (died 1790)
Oil on canvas: 74.3 x 61.6
With inscription
Reverse: signed and dated 1773
Bequest of Miss W. M. Fullerton 1936
NG 1837

John Thomas SETON
(active 1761–1806) Scottish
Katherine Paterson, Lady Walkinshaw (known as
Lady Burrowfield) (c. 1683–1780)
Oil on canvas: 76.2 x 63.5
Reverse: signed and dated 1776
Purchased 1936
NG 1840

John Thomas SETON
(active 1761–1806) Scottish
Mrs Smith (born c. 1690)
Oil on canvas: 75 x 62.2
Reverse: inscribed, signed and dated 1776
Purchased 1936
NG 1841

Georges SEURAT
(1859–91) French
A Study for 'Une Baignade'
Oil on panel: 15.9 x 25
With signature
Presented by Sir Alexander Maitland in memory
of his wife Rosalind 1960
NG 2222

Georges SEURAT
(1859–91) French
La Luzerne, Saint-Denis
Oil on canvas: 65.3 x 81.3
Signed
Purchased with the aid of the National Art
Collections Fund, a Treasury Grant and the family
of Roger Fry 1973
NG 2324

William Craig SHIRREFF
(1786–1805) Scottish
Mary Queen of Scots Escaping from Loch Leven Castle
Oil on canvas: 77.2 x 92.4
Presented by Mrs Fairgrieve 1963
NG 2255

William SIMSON
(1800–47) Scottish
Solway Moss: Evening
Oil on canvas: 66.7 x 94
Signed and dated 1830
Purchased by the RSA 1853;
transferred and presented 1910
NG 308

William SIMSON
(1800–47) Scottish
A Scene in Holland
Oil on panel: 24.1 x 39.4
Signed and dated 1828
Presented by Mrs Hugh William Williams 1860
NG 368

William SIMSON
(1800–47) Scottish
Twelfth of August
Oil on panel: 26 x 41.3
Presented by Mrs Hugh William Williams 1860
NG 369

William SIMSON
(1800–47) Scottish
Passage Boats Becalmed on the Maas at Dort
Oil on panel: 29.2 x 42.5
Purchased by the RI for the National Gallery
of Scotland 1867
NG 533

William SIMSON
(1800–47) Scottish
A Goatherd's Cottage
Oil on panel: 50 x 68.5
Signed and dated 1832
Transferred and presented by the RSA 1910
NG 609

William SIMSON
(1800–47) Scottish
A Dog's Head
Oil on canvas: 62.5 x 53.1
Bequest of Mary Hamilton Campbell, Baroness
Ruthven 1885
NG 708

Alexander Garden SINCLAIR
(1859–1930) Scottish
Horses Harrowing
Oil on canvas: 40 x 50.2
Signed with initials
Bequest of Mrs Louisa Hope Sinclair 1954
NG 2175

Elisabetta SIRANI
(1638–65) Italian
The Infant St John the Baptist in the Wilderness
Oil on canvas: 75.5 x 62
Signed and dated 1664
Purchased by the RI 1831; transferred 1859
NG 79

Alfred SISLEY
(1839–99) French
Molesey Weir, Hampton Court
Oil on canvas: 51.1 x 68.8
Signed and dated 1874
Presented by Sir Alexander Maitland in memory
of his wife Rosalind 1960
NG 2235

Alfred SISLEY
(1839–99) French
The Seine at Suresnes
Oil on canvas: 46.4 x 65.3
Signed and dated 1880
Presented by Mrs Isabel M. Traill 1979
NG 2386

John SMIBERT
(1688–1751) Scottish
*Colonel George Douglas, later 12th Earl
of Morton (1662–1738)*
Oil on canvas: 76.2 x 63.5
Signed and dated 1727
Purchased with the aid of the Annie H. Wilson
Bequest Fund 1959
NG 2212

Frans SNYDERS
(1579–1657) Flemish
Mischievous Monkeys
Oil on canvas: 99.6 x 117.5
Purchased by the RI for the National Gallery
of Scotland 1867
NG 532

After Frans SNYDERS
(1579–1657) Flemish
A Bear Hunt
Oil on canvas: 157 x 203
Purchased by the RI 1840; transferred 1859
NG 80

Andrea SOLDI
(*c.* 1703–71) Italian
Portrait of a Gentleman
Oil on canvas: 110.5 x 87.6
Purchased 1887
NG 795

Andrew SOMERVILLE
(1806–34) Scottish
Cottage Children
Oil on canvas: 35.5 x 30.2
Signed and dated 1830
Presented by William Nelson to the RSA 1887;
transferred and presented 1910
NG 805

SPANISH School
(17th century)
A Boy Drinking from a Flask
Oil on canvas: 45 x 37.5
Bequest of Lady Murray of Henderland 1861
NG 432

James STARK
(1794–1859) English
Gowbarrow Park
Oil on panel: 21.6 x 27.6
Purchased by the RI 1827; transferred 1859
NG 311

Jan STEEN
(1625/26–1679) Dutch
A School for Boys and Girls
Oil on canvas: 81.7 x 108.6
Purchased by Private Treaty with the aid
of the National Heritage Memorial Fund 1984
NG 2421

After Matthias STOM
(1598/1600–51) Dutch
A Man with a Jug and a Girl with a Viol
Oil on canvas: 91.4 x 78.7
Purchased 1920
NG 1446

William STOTT
(1857–1900) English
T. Millie Dow (1848–1919)
Oil on canvas: 106.5 x 81.5
Inscribed, signed and dated 1882
Bequest of Allan McLean 1928
NG 1692

Pierre SUBLEYRAS
(1699–1749) French
The Crucifixion of St Peter
Oil on canvas: 46.7 x 31
Purchased with the aid of the National Art
Collections Fund 1995
NG 2635

John Macallan SWAN
(1847–1910) English
Matthijs (or Matthew) Maris (1839–1917)
Oil on canvas: 52 x 41.3
Presented by Mrs Mary Swan
and Miss Mary Swan 1941
NG 1951

John SYME
(1795–1861) Scottish
*Portrait of Two Boys, called the Artist's Twin
Brothers*
Oil on canvas: 90.8 x 69.8
Presented by Miss Ella S. Boswell 1950
NG 2124

John SYME
(1795–1861) Scottish
The Artist's Sister (Maria Syme, 1793–1868)
Oil on canvas: 75 x 63.5
Presented by Miss Ella S. Boswell 1950
NG 2125

Attributed to Carlo Antonio TAVELLA
(1668–1738) Italian
Landscape
Oil on canvas: 62.3 x 85.8
Purchased by the RI 1830; transferred 1859
NG 88

David TENIERS the Younger
(1610–90) Flemish
Boors Drinking
Oil on panel: 37.5 x 27
Purchased 1891
NG 823

Pietro TESTA
(1612–50) Italian
The Adoration of the Shepherds
Oil on canvas: 88.3 x 125.5
Purchased with the aid of the National Art
Collections Fund 1973
NG 2325

After Pietro TESTA
(1612–50) Italian
The Triumph of Painting
Oil on canvas: 83.5 x 104.5
Presented by Miss Armide Oppé through
the National Art Collections Fund 1973
NG 2326

Revd John THOMSON
(1778–1840) Scottish
Robert the Bruce's Castle of Turnberry
Oil on canvas: 80.7 x 121.9
Commissioned by the RI in 1828; transferred 1859
NG 316

Revd John THOMSON
(1778–1840) Scottish
Landscape Composition
Oil on canvas: 50.8 x 76.2
Presented by Mrs Hugh William Williams 1860
NG 372

Revd John THOMSON
(1778–1840) Scottish
On the Firth of Clyde
Oil on canvas: 63.5 x 96.5
Bequest of Professor James Pillans 1863
NG 461

Revd John THOMSON
(1778–1840) Scottish
Ravensheugh Castle
Oil on canvas: 64.2 x 97.8
Bequest of Professor James Pillans 1863
NG 462

Revd John THOMSON
(1778–1840) Scottish
The Trossachs
Oil on canvas: 63.5 x 127
Bequest of Professor James Pillans 1863
NG 463

Revd John THOMSON
(1778–1840) Scottish
Trees on the Bank of a Stream
Oil on canvas: 28 x 22.2
Bequest of Professor James Pillans 1863
NG 464

Revd John THOMSON
(1778–1840) Scottish
Aberlady Bay
Oil on canvas: 64.2 x 94.6
Bequest of Katherine Munro, Lady Steuart
of Allanbank 1867
NG 556

Revd John THOMSON
(1778–1840) Scottish
Wooded Landscape
Oil on panel: 30.2 x 24.1
Purchased 1905
NG 929

Revd John THOMSON
(1778–1840) Scottish
The Castle on the Rock
Oil on canvas: 35.6 x 48.3
Presented by Alexander Wood Inglis 1919
NG 1228

Revd John THOMSON
(1778–1840) Scottish
Fast Castle
Oil on panel: 51 x 76.2
Bequest of Alexander Wood Inglis 1929
NG 1727

Revd John THOMSON
(1778–1840) Scottish
A Cliff Scene (Fast Castle)
Oil on canvas: 41.6 x 49.5
Purchased 1936
NG 1864

Revd John THOMSON
(1778–1840) Scottish
Fast Castle from below (companion-piece
to NG 2412)
Oil on canvas: 76.2 x 105.4
Purchased 1946
NG 2039

Revd John THOMSON
(1778–1840) Scottish
Landscape Composition
Oil on panel: 36.8 x 48.3
Purchased 1957
NG 2191

Revd John THOMSON
(1778–1840) Scottish
The Artist's Son (Dr Francis Thomson, 1814–58)
Oil on millboard: 35.6 x 25.5
Presented by Mrs Margaret Luard 1961
NG 2249

Revd John THOMSON
(1778–1840) Scottish
Edinburgh from Corstorphine Hill
Oil on panel: 34.9 x 48.3
With inscription
Purchased 1963
NG 2263

Revd John THOMSON
(1778–1840) Scottish
A View South of Edinburgh
Oil on paper laid on panel: 26.7 x 32.4
With inscription
Purchased 1963
NG 2264

Revd John THOMSON
(1778–1840) Scottish
Glen Altrive, Selkirkshire
Oil on canvas: 44.5 x 59.7
Purchased 1963
NG 2265

Revd John THOMSON
(1778–1840) Scottish
Fast Castle from above (companion-piece
to NG 2039)
Oil on canvas: 77 x 106.4
Signed with initials and dated 1823
Purchased 1981
NG 2412

Giovanni Battista TIEPOLO
(1696–1770) Italian
The Meeting of Anthony and Cleopatra
Oil on canvas: 66.8 x 38.4
Purchased by the RI 1845; transferred 1867
NG 91

Giovanni Battista TIEPOLO
(1696–1770) Italian
The Finding of Moses
Oil on canvas: 202 x 342 (cut down)
Presented to the RI by Robert Clouston 1845;
transferred 1859
NG 92

Jacopo TINTORETTO (Robusti)
(1518–94) Italian
The Head of a Man with a Red Beard
Oil on canvas: 36 x 27.2 (fragment)
Bequest of Mary Hamilton Campbell,
Baroness Ruthven 1885
NG 689

Jacopo TINTORETTO (Robusti)
(1518–94) Italian
Christ Carried to the Tomb
Oil on canvas: 164 x 127.5 (cut down)
Purchased by Private Treaty with the aid
of the National Heritage Memorial Fund 1984
NG 2419

Jacopo TINTORETTO (Robusti)
(1518–94) Italian
Portrait of a Venetian
Oil on canvas: 74.5 x 61.8
Lent by the Duke of Sutherland 1947

Jacopo TINTORETTO (Robusti) and Studio
(1518–94) Italian
A Venetian Family Presented to the Madonna
by St Lawrence and a Bishop Saint
Oil on canvas: 223.7 x 173.2
Purchased 1952
NG 2161

Studio of Jacopo TINTORETTO (Robusti)
(1518–94) Italian
Portrait of a Man
Oil on canvas: 85 x 73.5
Purchased by the RI 1845; transferred 1867
NG 99

Follower of Jacopo TINTORETTO (Robusti)
(1518–94) Italian
Summer
Oil on canvas: 116 x 95.5
Purchased by the RI 1830; transferred 1859
NG 96

Follower of Jacopo TINTORETTO (Robusti)
(1518–94) Italian
Spring
Oil on canvas: 116 x 95.5
Purchased by the RI 1830; transferred 1859
NG 97

Follower of Jacopo TINTORETTO (Robusti)
(1518–94) Italian
Winter
Oil on canvas: 115.5 x 95.5
Purchased by the RI 1830; transferred 1859
NG 98

TITIAN (Tiziano Vecellio)
(active 1511 – died 1576) Italian
*The Virgin and Child with St John the Baptist and
an Unidentified Male Saint*
Oil on canvas, transferred from panel: 62.7 x 93
Lent by the Duke of Sutherland 1945

TITIAN (Tiziano Vecellio)
(active 1511 – died 1576) Italian
The Three Ages of Man
Oil on canvas: 90 x 150.7
Lent by the Duke of Sutherland 1945

TITIAN (Tiziano Vecellio)
(active 1511 – died 1576) Italian
Venus Anadyomene (Venus Rising from the Sea)
Oil on canvas: 75.8 x 57.6
Lent by the Duke of Sutherland 1945

TITIAN (Tiziano Vecellio)
(active 1511 – died 1576) Italian
Diana and Actaeon
Oil on canvas: 184.5 x 202.2
Lent by the Duke of Sutherland 1945

TITIAN (Tiziano Vecellio)
(active 1511 – died 1576) Italian
Diana and Callisto
Oil on canvas: 187 x 204.5
Signed
Lent by the Duke of Sutherland 1945

After TITIAN (Tiziano Vecellio)
(active 1511 – died 1576) Italian
A Bacchanal: The Andrians
Oil on canvas: 168 x 218.5
Purchased by the RSA 1853;
transferred and presented 1910
NG 103

Imitator of TITIAN (Tiziano Vecellio)
(active 1511 – died 1576) Italian
Portrait of a Man
Oil on panel: 71 x 57.7
Purchased by the RI 1830; transferred 1859
NG 104

James A. S. TORRANCE
(1859–1916) Scottish
The Pet Pigeon
Oil on canvas: 45.7 x 38.7
Presented by Mrs Louise Torrance 1917
NG 1206

James A. S. TORRANCE
(1859–1916) Scottish
Dimples
Oil on canvas: 30.5 x 25.5
Bequest of Sir James Lewis Caw 1951
NG 2146

Studio of Giovanni TOSCANI
(active 1423 – died 1430) Italian
Cassone with Scenes from Boccaccio's 'Decameron'
Tempera on panel: 82 x 182 x 60 (cassone);
41.9 x 142 (painted front panel)
Presented by Dr John Warrack 1929
NG 1738

Phoebe Anna TRAQUAIR
(1852–1936) Scottish
The Progress of a Soul: The Entrance
Silk and gold thread embroidered on linen:
180.7 x 71.2
With embroidered signature in monogram
and dated 1895
Bequest of the artist 1936
NG 1865 A

Phoebe Anna TRAQUAIR
(1852–1936) Scottish
The Progress of a Soul: The Stress
Silk and gold thread embroidered on linen:
180.7 x 71.2
With embroidered signature in monogram
and dated 1897
Bequest of the artist 1936
NG 1865 B

Phoebe Anna TRAQUAIR
(1852–1936) Scottish
The Progress of a Soul: Despair
Silk and gold thread embroidered on linen:
184.7 x 74.9
With embroidered signature in monogram
Bequest of the artist 1936
NG 1865 C

Phoebe Anna TRAQUAIR
(1852–1936) Scottish
The Progress of a Soul: The Victory
Silk and gold thread embroidered on linen:
188.2 x 74.2
With embroidered signature in monogram
and dated 1902
Bequest of the artist 1936
NG 1865 D

Phoebe Anna TRAQUAIR
(1852–1936) Scottish
Pan
Oil on panel: 175.3 x 82.6
Signed in monogram and dated 1912
Bequest of the artist 1936
NG 1866

Phoebe Anna TRAQUAIR
(1852–1936) Scottish
*Studies for the Decoration of the first Mortuary
Chapel, the Royal Hospital for Sick Children,
Edinburgh*
(see next three items for individual subjects)
Oil and gold leaf on canvas
Inscribed
Bequest of the artist 1936
NG 1867

Phoebe Anna TRAQUAIR
(1852–1936) Scottish
*A Study for the Decoration of the first Mortuary
Chapel, the Royal Hospital for Sick Children,
Edinburgh: The Virgin and Child with Angels*
(centre panel)
Oil and gold leaf on canvas: 25.1 x 21.9
Inscribed
Bequest of the artist 1936
NG 1867 A

Phoebe Anna TRAQUAIR
(1852–1936) Scottish
*A Study for the Decoration of the first Mortuary
Chapel, the Royal Hospital for Sick Children,
Edinburgh: An Angel Escorting another Angel
towards Heaven* (left panel)
Oil on canvas: 24.8 x 20
Bequest of the artist 1936
NG 1867 B

Phoebe Anna TRAQUAIR
(1852–1936) Scottish
*A Study for the Decoration of the first Mortuary
Chapel, the Royal Hospital for Sick Children,
Edinburgh: The Holy Spirit Awakening the Spirit
of the Deceased* (right panel)
Oil on canvas: 24.8 x 20
Bequest of the artist 1936
NG 1867 C

Phoebe Anna TRAQUAIR
(1852–1936) Scottish
*'For So He Giveth His Beloved Sleep': Fragment of
a Mural from the Mortuary Chapel, the Royal
Hospital for Sick Children, Edinburgh*
Oil on plaster, lath and brick: 41.2 x 34
Inscribed and signed in monogram
Bequest of the artist 1936
NG 1868

Phoebe Anna TRAQUAIR
(1852–1936) Scottish
The Shepherd Boy
Oil on canvas: 19.8 x 24.5
Signed in monogram and dated 1891
Bequest of the artist 1936
NG 1869

Phoebe Anna TRAQUAIR
(1852–1936) Scottish
Triptych: *Motherhood*
Oil on panel, in a repoussée copper frame,
with inset lapidary and cloisonné enamel panels
on exterior of wings: 22.3 x 18.2 (centre);
22.3 x 9.3 (wings)
Signed in monogram and dated 1902
Bequest of the artist 1936
NG 1871

Phoebe Anna TRAQUAIR
(1852–1936) Scottish
The Awakening
Oil on panel: 62.2 x 151
Inscribed, signed in monogram and dated 1904
Bequest of Mrs Deirdre Inches Carr 1996
NG 2655

Constant TROYON
(1810–65) French
Cattle Grazing in Touraine
Oil on canvas: 81.5 x 117.5
Signed
Bequest of Hugh A. Laird 1911
NG 1033

Constant TROYON
(1810–65) French
Return from Work
Oil on canvas: 64.8 x 81.3
Signed
Bequest of Hugh A. Laird 1911
NG 1034

Constant TROYON
(1810–65) French
Sheep and Shepherd
Oil on panel: 34.3 x 26
Signed
Bequest of Dr John Kirkhope 1920
NG 1466

Joseph Mallord William TURNER
(1775–1851) English
Somer Hill, Tonbridge
Oil on canvas: 92 x 122
Purchased with the aid of the Cowan Smith
Bequest Fund 1922
NG 1614

TUSCAN School
(14th century)
Triptych. Centre: *The Virgin and Child Enthroned.*
Left wing: *The Nativity; The Angel of the*
Annunciation. Right wing: *The Crucifixion; The*
Virgin Annunciate
Tempera and gold on panel: 47.5 x 22.8 (centre);
51.3 x 12 (left wing); 51.3 x 11.2 (right wing)
Purchased 1942
NG 1958

UNKNOWN
(17th century)
Portrait of a Man, called Robert, Mester Erskine,
probably Colonel Alexander Erskine of
Cambuskenneth (died 1640)
Oil on canvas: 230 x 150
With inscription and date 1627
Purchased 1942
NG 1973

Grigor URQUHART
(*c.* 1797– after 1846) Scottish
The Transfiguration (after Raphael)
Oil on canvas: 414 x 285
Purchased by the RI 1827; transferred 1867
NG 66

Diego VELÁZQUEZ
(1599–1660) Spanish
An Old Woman Cooking Eggs
Oil on canvas: 100.5 x 119.5
Dated 1618
Purchased with the aid of the National Art
Collections Fund and a Treasury Grant 1955
NG 2180

After Diego VELÁZQUEZ
(1599–1660) Spanish
King Philip IV of Spain (1605–65)
Oil on canvas: 51.1 x 46
Purchased 1923
NG 1625

Willem van de VELDE the Elder
(1611–93) Dutch
*A Sea-piece with a Dutch Merchant Ship
and a Swedish Flute*
Pen and brush on panel: 60.5 x 83.6
Signed
Presented by Hew Hamilton Dalrymple 1906;
transferred from the Department of Prints
and Drawings 1987
NG 933

Imitator of Willem van de VELDE the Younger
(1633–1707) Dutch
Ships in a Calm Sea
Oil on panel: 36.8 x 49.9
Bequest of Miss Alice Anne White 1941
NG 1947

VENETIAN School
(16th century)
Portrait of a Gentleman
Oil on canvas: 127 x 98
Purchased by the RI 1830; transferred 1859
NG 3

VENETIAN School
(16th century)
An Archer
Oil on panel: 53.5 x 41.5
Bequest of Mary Hamilton Campbell,
Baroness Ruthven 1885
NG 690

VENETIAN School
(16th century)
A Scholar with an Inkstand
Oil on canvas: 89 x 109.5
Inscribed
Bequest of Mary Hamilton Campbell,
Baroness Ruthven 1885
NG 704

Gaspar Pieter VERBRUGGEN the Younger
(1664–1730) Flemish
Still Life with Fruit and Flowers
Oil on canvas: 40 x 32.5
Signed
Bequest of Mrs Nisbet Hamilton Ogilvy
of Biel 1921
NG 1516

Gaspar Pieter VERBRUGGEN the Younger
(1664–1730) Flemish
Still Life with Fruit and Flowers
Oil on canvas: 40.3 x 32.8
Signed
Bequest of Mrs Nisbet Hamilton Ogilvy
of Biel 1921
NG 1517

Nicolaas VERKOLJE
(1673–1746) Dutch
Two Vestal Virgins
Oil on panel: 45.7 x 42.7
Purchased 1993
NG 2563

Johannes VERMEER
(1632–75) Dutch
Christ in the House of Martha and Mary
Oil on canvas: 158.5 x 141.5
Signed
Presented by the sons of W. A. Coats in memory of
their father 1927
NG 1670

Follower of Joseph VERNET
(1714–89) French
The Italian Gondola
Oil on canvas: 73.5 x 97.5
Bequest of Sir Claude Phillips 1924
NG 1637

Paolo VERONESE (Caliari)
(*c.* 1528–88) Italian
Mars and Venus
Oil on canvas: 165.2 x 126.5
Purchased by the RI 1859; transferred 1867
NG 339

Paolo VERONESE (Caliari)
(*c.* 1528–88) Italian
St Anthony Abbot as Patron of a Kneeling Donor
Oil on canvas: 198.5 x 117.8 (fragment)
Purchased 1913
NG 1139

Attributed to Andrea del VERROCCHIO
and Workshop
(*c.* 1435–88) Italian
The Virgin and Child ('The Ruskin Madonna')
Canvas transferred from panel: 106.7 x 76.3
Purchased with the aid of the National Art
Collections Fund and the Pilgrim Trust 1975
NG 2338

Antoine VESTIER
(1740–1824) French
The Artist's Daughter (Marie-Nicole Vestier)
Oil on canvas: 93.1 x 74
Signed and dated 1785
Bequest of Miss K. M. Richardson 1994
NG 2588

VITALE da Bologna (Vitale d'Aimo de' Cavalli)
(active 1334–59/61) Italian
*The Adoration of the Kings with St Ursula
and St Catherine of Alexandria*
Tempera and gold on panel: 60.4 x 38.6
Purchased 1908
NG 952

Antoine VOLLON
(1833–1900) French
The Silver Vase
Oil on panel: 24 x 18
Signed
Bequest of Dr John Kirkhope 1920
NG 1467

After Simon VOUET
(1590–1649) French
Venus and Adonis
Oil on copper: 21.2 x 17.7
Purchased 1891
NG 826

Richard WAITT
(active 1708 – died 1732) Scottish
Still Life
Oil on canvas: 59 x 77.5
Signed and dated 1724
Purchased 1978
NG 2366

William WALLS
(1860–1942) Scottish
The Artist's Mother (Mrs James Walls)
Oil on canvas: 90.8 x 73
Signed
Presented by Mrs Elizabeth M. Walls 1944
NG 1982

Goffredo WALS
(*c.* 1595– *c.* 1638) German
Landscape with Christ and (?) St Peter
Oil on copper: 28.5 (circular)
Purchased with the aid of the National Art
Collections Fund 1990
NG 2516

Edward Arthur WALTON
(1860–1922) Scottish
The Ford, New Abbey
Oil on canvas: 78.8 x 101.9
Signed
Presented by Henry Ballantyne 1925
NG 1655

Edward Arthur WALTON
(1860–1922) Scottish
*The Artist's Mother (Elizabeth Balfour Nicolson,
Mrs Jackson Walton)*
Oil on canvas: 129 x 103.7
With inscription
Reverse: with inscription and date 1885
Presented by Mrs Dorothy Walton 1977
NG 2348

Edward Arthur WALTON
(1860–1922) Scottish
Bluette
Oil on canvas: 76.2 x 87.6
Signed
Purchased 1981
NG 2408

James WARD
(1769–1859) English
The Eildon Hills and the Tweed
Oil on panel: 103 x 173
Signed in monogram and dated 1807
Bequest of Sir Theophilus Biddulph 1948;
received 1969
NG 2306

James WARD
(1769–1859) English
Melrose Abbey, the Pavilion in the Distance
Oil on panel: 103 x 173
Signed
Bequest of Sir Theophilus Biddulph 1948;
received 1969
NG 2307

Thomas WARRENDER
(active 1673–1713) Scottish
Still Life
Oil on canvas: 59.1 x 74.3
Purchased 1980
NG 2404

George WATSON
(1767–1837) Scottish
Sir Benjamin West (1738–1820)
Oil on canvas: 90.2 x 71.1
Inscribed and signed
Presented by the artist's son, William
Smellie Watson, to the RSA 1859;
transferred and presented 1910
NG 319

George WATSON
(1767–1837) Scottish
*Mary Augusta Riddell, later Mrs Cunliffe
(1823–79)*
Oil on canvas: 143 x 114.3
Presented by the Revd Henry Cunliffe 1886
NG 720

George WATSON
(1767–1837) Scottish
Self-portrait (companion-piece to NG 927)
Oil on canvas: 90.2 x 71.1
Presented by Arthur Sanderson 1905
NG 926

George WATSON
(176/–1837) Scottish
The Artist's Wife (Rebecca Smellie)
(companion-piece to NG 926)
Oil on canvas: 90.2 x 71.1
Presented by Arthur Sanderson 1905
NG 927

George WATSON
(1767–1837) Scottish
Zoe de Bellecourt, later Mrs Stafford
Oil on canvas: 129 x 98.4
Presented by Major-General Sir Theodore
Fraser 1937
NG 1885

William Stewart WATSON
(1800–70) Scottish
Don Quixote Tilting at a Windmill
Oil on canvas: 68.6 x 92.1
Presented to the RI by the artist 1832;
transferred 1859
NG 322

Jean-Antoine WATTEAU
(1684–1721) French
*The Robber of the Sparrow's Nest ('Le Dénicheur
de Moineaux')*
Oil on paper laid on canvas laid on panel:
22.6 x 18.5
Presented by Mrs Hugh William Williams 1860
NG 370

Jean-Antoine WATTEAU
(1684–1721) French
Fêtes Vénitiennes
Oil on canvas: 55.9 x 45.7
Bequest of Lady Murray of Henderland 1861
NG 439

George Frederic WATTS
(1817–1904) English
Mischief
Oil on panel: 198 x 101.6
Presented by the artist's executors 1906
NG 932

George Frederic WATTS
(1817–1904) English
Caroline Muriel Callander, later Mrs Baird
(c. 1861–1932)
Oil on canvas: 61 x 50.8
Bequest of Mrs C. M. Baird 1933
NG 1788

George Frederic WATTS
(1817–1904) English
Theophilos Kairis (1784–1853)
Oil on canvas: 76.2 x 63.5
Signed
Presented by Miss Daphne Ionides 1946
NG 2041

Jan Baptist WEENIX
(1621– before 1663) Dutch
Figures near a Seaport
Oil on canvas: 66.7 x 72.4
Purchased by the RI 1831; transferred 1859
NG 51

Jan WEENIX
(c. 1642–1719) Dutch
Landscape with a Huntsman and Dead Game
(Allegory of the Sense of Smell)
Oil on canvas: 344 x 323
Signed and dated 1697
Purchased 1990
NG 2523

Hendrik Johannes WEISSENBRUCH
(1824–1903) Dutch
Near Dordrecht
Oil on panel: 23.2 x 41.3
Signed
Bequest of Hugh A. Laird 1911
NG 1062

Benjamin WEST
(1738–1820) American
Alexander III of Scotland Rescued from the Fury
of a Stag by the Intrepidity of Colin Fitzgerald
Oil on canvas: 366 x 521
Signed and dated 1786
Purchased with the aid of the National Heritage
Memorial Fund, the National Art Collections
Fund (William Lang Bequest), Ross & Cromarty
District Council and Denis F. Ward 1987
NG 2448

Attributed to Francis WHEATLEY
(1747–1801) English
Portrait of a Boy, called John Cumming
Oil on canvas: 38.1 x 30.2
Bequest of Mrs I. M. Cumming 1965
NG 2272

James Abbot McNeill WHISTLER
(1834–1903) American
An Arrangement in Grey and Green. Portrait
of John James Cowan (1846–1936)
Oil on canvas: 95.5 x 51
Presented by Miss Birnie Philip, associating
Mr Cowan's name with the gift 1930
NG 1744

Jan WIJNANTS
(active 1643 – died 1684) Dutch
Landscape with Figures
Oil on canvas: 62.6 x 73.7
Signed and dated 1665
Bequest of Miss Alice Anne White 1941
NG 1945

Sir David WILKIE
(1785–1841) Scottish
*John Knox Dispensing the Sacrament
at Calder House*
Oil on panel: 123.2 x 165 (unfinished)
Purchased by the RSA 1842;
transferred and presented 1910
NG 323

Sir David WILKIE
(1785–1841) Scottish
*The Artist's Sister (Helen Wilkie,
later Mrs William Hunter, 1793–1870)*
Oil on panel: 27.3 x 21.6
Bequest of Dr William Hunter 1871
NG 585

Sir David WILKIE
(1785–1841) Scottish
A Scene from Ramsay's 'The Gentle Shepherd'
Oil on panel: 30.5 x 41.3
Purchased 1898
NG 839

Sir David WILKIE
(1785–1841) Scottish
*The Preaching of John Knox before the Lords
of the Congregation 10th June 1559*
Oil on canvas: 46 x 54.7
Signed and dated 1832
Purchased 1907
NG 950

Sir David WILKIE
(1785–1841) Scottish
Sheepwashing
Oil on panel: 90 x 137
Bequest of Hugh A. Laird 1911
NG 1032

Sir David WILKIE
(1785–1841) Scottish
The Bride at her Toilet on the Day of her Wedding
Oil on canvas: 100 x 125
Inscribed, signed and dated 1838
Purchased 1920
NG 1445

Sir David WILKIE
(1785–1841) Scottish
Pitlessie Fair
Oil on canvas: 61.5 x 110.5
Signed and dated 1804
Purchased 1921
NG 1527

Sir David WILKIE
(1785–1841) Scottish
Duncan Gray
Oil on panel: 38 x 32.6
Purchased 1928
NG 1720

Sir David WILKIE
(1785–1841) Scottish
The Letter of Introduction
Oil on panel: 61 x 50.2
Signed and dated 1813
Purchased 1938
NG 1890

Sir David WILKIE
(1785–1841) Scottish
The Artist's Niece (Sophia Wilkie,
later Mrs James Winfield)
Oil on canvas: 60 x 45
Signed and dated 1829
Presented by Miss M. Florence Nightingale 1948
NG 2103

Sir David WILKIE
(1785–1841) Scottish
Josephine and the Fortune-teller
Oil on canvas: 211 x 158
Signed and dated 1837
Purchased 1949
NG 2114

Sir David WILKIE
(1785–1841) Scottish
The Irish Whiskey Still
Oil on panel: 119.4 x 158
Signed and dated 1840
Purchased 1950
NG 2130

Sir David WILKIE
(1785–1841) Scottish
*A Study for 'John Knox Dispensing
the Sacrament at Calder House'* (NG 323)
Oil on panel: 45.1 x 61
Presented by John M. Naylor 1953
NG 2172

Sir David WILKIE
(1785–1841) Scottish
The Artist's Parents
*(The Revd David Wilkie, 1738–1812 and his Wife
Isabella Lister, 1763–1824)*
Oil on panel: 25.5 x 20
Purchased 1953
NG 2173

Sir David WILKIE
(1785–1841) Scottish
A Dog Facing Right
Oil on panel: 7.6 x 10.5
Presented by the Earl of Leven and Melville 1949
NG 2196

Sir David WILKIE
(1785–1841) Scottish
A Dog Facing Left
Oil on panel: 7.6 x 11.1
Presented by the Earl of Leven and Melville 1949
NG 2197

Sir David WILKIE
(1785–1841) Scottish
Sheep
Oil on panel: 5.4 x 8.6
Presented by the Earl of Leven and Melville 1949
NG 2198

Sir David WILKIE
(1785–1841) Scottish
A Study for 'Duncan Gray' (NG 1720)
Oil on panel: 13 x 9.9
Reverse: with inscription
Presented by Ian Hutchison 1968
NG 2302

Sir David WILKIE
(1785–1841) Scottish
*The Confessional (Pilgrims Confessing
in the Basilica of St Peter's)*
Oil on canvas: 48.2 x 38.6
Signed and dated 1827
Purchased 1972
NG 2315

Sir David WILKIE
(1785–1841) Scottish
Distraining for Rent
Oil on panel: 81.3 x 123
Signed and dated 1815
Purchased 1975
NG 2337

Sir David WILKIE
(1785–1841) Scottish
General Sir David Baird Discovering the Body
of Sultan Tippoo Sahib after having Captured
Seringapatam, on the 4th May, 1799
Oil on canvas: 348.5 x 267.9
Signed
Presented by Irvine Chalmers Watson 1985
NG 2430

Sir David WILKIE
(1785–1841) Scottish
William Chalmers Bethune (1744–1807),
his Wife Isobel Morison (1760–1850) and their
Daughter Isabella (died 1818)
Oil on canvas: 125.7 x 102.9
Signed and dated 1804
Purchased with the Barrogill Keith Bequest Fund,
with additional funding from the Rutherford
and Laird McDougall Funds and the Cowan Smith
Bequest Fund 1985
NG 2433

After Sir David WILKIE
(1785–1841) Scottish
The Blind Fiddler
Oil on canvas: 25.7 x 37.5
With signature and date 1806
Purchased 1929
NG 1725

After Sir David WILKIE
(1785–1841) Scottish
The Jew's Harp
Oil on panel: 24.1 x 16.5
Purchased 1936
NG 1842

Hugh William WILLIAMS
(1773–1829) Scottish
Castle Urquhart, Loch Ness
Oil on canvas: 97.5 x 131
Presented by Mrs Hugh William Williams 1860
NG 371

S. WILLIAMS
(19th century) Scottish
St Peter and St Paul (after Guido Reni)
Oil on canvas: 201 x 137
Presented by Henry Drummond to the Board
of Manufactures; transferred 1859
NG 43

Andrew WILSON
(1780–1848) Scottish
A View of Tivoli
Oil on canvas: 28.6 x 43.8
Purchased by the RSA 1851;
transferred and presented 1910
NG 326

Andrew WILSON
(1780–1848) Scottish
A View of Burntisland
Oil on canvas: 77.9 x 119
Bequest of Duncan MacNeill, Lord Colonsay 1874
NG 605

Andrew WILSON
(1780–1848) Scottish
Off Porto Fino
Oil on panel: 27.5 x 41.2
Reverse: with inscription
Purchased 1940
NG 1924

Andrew WILSON
(1780–1848) Scottish
Evening in the Bay of Genoa
Oil on canvas: 116.7 x 170.4
Purchased 1990
NG 2520

John WILSON
(1774–1855) Scottish
A Coastal Scene between Nieuport and Ostend
Oil on panel: 27 x 37.1
Reverse: with inscription and date 1816
Purchased by the RSA 1856;
transferred and presented 1910
NG 328

John WILSON
(1774–1855) Scottish
A Ferry Boat on the Maas
Oil on canvas: 74.9 x 105.1
Signed and dated 1828
Purchased by the RSA 1856;
transferred and presented 1910
NG 329

John James WILSON
(1818–75) Scottish
A Sea-piece
Oil on canvas: 51.5 x 104.5
Signed with initials and dated 1852
Presented by George R. MacDougall 1902
NG 902

Richard WILSON
(1713/14–1782) Welsh
A River Scene with a Castle and Figures
Oil on canvas: 85.1 x 127
Bequest of Mrs Mary Veitch to the RSA 1875;
transferred and presented 1910
NG 620

Imitator of Richard WILSON
(1713/14–1782) Welsh
Lake Albano
Oil on canvas: 31 x 43.2
Purchased 1928
NG 1714

Sir James Lawton WINGATE
(1846–1924) Scottish
Sundown, Arran
Oil on canvas: 41.6 x 47.6
Signed
Bequest of Dr John Kirkhope 1920
NG 1487

Sir James Lawton WINGATE
(1846–1924) Scottish
Ash Trees in Spring
Oil on canvas: 43.2 x 31.1
Signed
Bequest of Dr John Kirkhope 1920
NG 1488

Sir James Lawton WINGATE
(1846–1924) Scottish
A Summer's Evening
Oil on canvas: 54.5 x 74.3
Signed and dated 1888
Bequest of Mrs T. Hall Cooper 1925
NG 1649

Sir James Lawton WINGATE
(1846–1924) Scottish
Golden Sunset
Oil on canvas: 30.8 x 40.8
Signed
Bequest of Alexander F. Roberts 1929
NG 1734

Sir James Lawton WINGATE
(1846–1924) Scottish
Sheepshearing
Oil on canvas: 89.5 x 115.6
Signed
Presented by Mrs Helen Wingate Thornton 1949
NG 2111

Sir James Lawton WINGATE
(1846–1924) Scottish
Harvest in Arran
Oil on canvas: 26 x 36.2
Signed
Bequest of Lady Caw 1950
NG 2123

Sir James Lawton WINGATE
(1846–1924) Scottish
Stormcloud, Muthill
Oil on millboard: 20.5 x 30.3
Signed
Bequest of Dr Robert A. Lillie 1977
NG 2358

Sir James Lawton WINGATE
(1846–1924) Scottish
Kilbrennan Sound
Oil on canvas: 35.3 x 45.6
Signed
Bequest of Dr Robert A. Lillie 1977
NG 2359

Peter de WINT
(1784–1849) English
A Distant View of Lincoln Cathedral
Oil on canvas: 108 x 163
Presented by Messrs Davidson and Syme 1932
NG 1776

John Crawford WINTOUR
(1825–82) Scottish
A Border Castle
Oil on canvas: 100.3 x 125.8
Bequest of Archibald Smith 1919
NG 1218

John Crawford WINTOUR
(1825–82) Scottish
Riverside Landscape
Oil on canvas: 43.5 x 61.3
Signed
Bequest of Dr John Kirkhope 1920
NG 1489

John Crawford WINTOUR
(1825–82) Scottish
On the Water of Leith
Oil on panel: 24.8 x 34
Bequest of Dr John Kirkhope 1920
NG 1490

John Crawford WINTOUR
(1825–82) Scottish
Moonlight, Blairlogie
Oil on millboard: 35.5 x 51.1
Bequest of Sir James Lewis Caw 1951
NG 2141

Emanuel de WITTE
(1615/17–1691/92) Dutch
The Interior of a Dutch Church
Oil on canvas: 190 x 162
Purchased 1909
NG 990

William YELLOWLEES
(1796–1855) Scottish
The Artist's Father (John Yellowlees, 1748–1831)
Oil on canvas laid on panel: 24.5 x 19.4
Presented by Mr and Mrs Michael Foley 1963
NG 2257

William YELLOWLEES
(1796–1855) Scottish
The Artist's Mother (Isabella Newton,
Mrs John Yellowlees, 1753–1825)
Oil on canvas laid on panel: 24.8 x 19.7
Presented by Mr and Mrs Michael Foley 1963
NG 2258

Attributed to Marco ZOPPO
(1432–78) Italian
Noli Me Tangere
Panel: 33.5 x 24.5
Purchased 1928
NG 1719

Francisco de ZURBARÁN
(1598–1664) Spanish
The Immaculate Conception with St Joachim
and St Anne
Oil on canvas: 255.5 x 177 (arched)
Purchased by the RI 1859; transferred 1867
NG 340

NUMERICAL INDEX

Works are listed in the order of their accession number with the names under which they appear in the Concise Catalogue.

NG 193	Robert GIBB		NG 440	Nicolas LANCRET
NG 198	John GRAHAM GILBERT		NG 441	Jean-Baptiste PATER
NG 204	Sir John Watson GORDON		NG 448	Thomas DUNCAN
NG 210	David Octavius HILL		NG 458	After Giovanni BELLINI
NG 213	Henry HOWARD		NG 459	Vicente CARDUCHO
NG 221	Robert Scott LAUDER		NG 460	William DYCE
NG 288	Horatio McCULLOCH		NG 461	Revd John THOMSON
NG 290	Jacob MORE		NG 462	Revd John THOMSON
NG 291	Alexander NASMYTH		NG 463	Revd John THOMSON
NG 293	Sir Joseph Noel PATON		NG 464	Revd John THOMSON
NG 294	Sir Joseph Noel PATON		NG 466	Thomas DUNCAN
NG 302	Sir Henry RAEBURN		NG 521	William DYCE
NG 304	David ROBERTS		NG 522	Sir Henry RAEBURN
NG 305	Sir John Baptiste de MEDINA		NG 529	Jan FYT
NG 308	William SIMSON		NG 530	Jan FYT
NG 311	James STARK		NG 532	Frans SNYDERS
NG 316	Revd John THOMSON		NG 533	William SIMSON
NG 319	George WATSON		NG 534	John PHILLIP
NG 322	William Stewart WATSON		NG 554	John MEDINA the Younger
NG 323	Sir David WILKIE		NG 556	Revd John THOMSON
NG 326	Andrew WILSON		NG 566	John PHILLIP
NG 328	John WILSON		NG 569	David MARTIN
NG 329	John WILSON		NG 570	John RUNCIMAN
NG 332	Thomas GAINSBOROUGH		NG 578	Alexander CHRISTIE
NG 338	Sir Joshua REYNOLDS		NG 579	After Jacob JORDAENS
NG 339	Paolo VERONESE		NG 585	Sir David WILKIE
NG 340	Francisco de ZURBARÁN		NG 586	Sir Edwin LANDSEER
NG 342	David SCOTT		NG 587	Horatio McCULLOCH
NG 368	William SIMSON		NG 589	Attributed to Patrick NASMYTH
NG 369	William SIMSON		NG 599	Robert HERDMAN
NG 370	Jean-Antoine WATTEAU		NG 600	After Salvator ROSA
NG 371	Hugh William WILLIAMS		NG 600 A	After Salvator ROSA
NG 372	Revd John THOMSON		NG 604	Thomas DUNCAN
NG 376	Hendrik van MINDERHOUT		NG 605	Andrew WILSON
NG 415	David ALLAN		NG 608	Sir George HARVEY
NG 416	Andrew GEDDES		NG 609	William SIMSON
NG 420	Sir Henry RAEBURN		NG 610	Sir Daniel MACNEE
NG 421	Edmund Thornton CRAWFORD		NG 612	David ALLAN
NG 423	William Home LIZARS		NG 619	Christian Wilhelm DIETRICH
NG 424	William Home LIZARS		NG 620	Richard WILSON
NG 427	Sir Joshua REYNOLDS		NG 621	Jacques COURTOIS
NG 429	Attributed to François BOUCHER		NG 622	After Salvator ROSA
NG 430	Allan RAMSAY		NG 623	Sir Henry RAEBURN
NG 431	William MARLOW		NG 624	James DRUMMOND
NG 432	SPANISH School		NG 625	James DRUMMOND
NG 433	Philippe MERCIER		NG 626	Sir Henry RAEBURN
NG 434	Philippe MERCIER		NG 627	Philippe MERCIER
NG 435	Jean-Baptiste GREUZE		NG 628	Philippe MERCIER
NG 436	Jean-Baptiste GREUZE		NG 630	Andrew GEDDES
NG 437	Jean-Baptiste GREUZE		NG 631	Andrew GEDDES
NG 438	After Jean-Baptiste GREUZE		NG 632	Robert Thorburn ROSS
NG 439	Jean-Antoine WATTEAU		NG 638	Studio of GIULIO Romano

NG 642	William BONNAR	NG 839	Sir David WILKIE
NG 645	FLORENTINE School	NG 843	David SCOTT
NG 646	Follower of LORENZO di Credi	NG 844	Attributed to David HODGSON
NG 647	Hendrick AVERCAMP	NG 845	Sir Henry RAEBURN
NG 648	John RUNCIMAN	NG 846	Sir Henry RAEBURN
NG 649	Sir John Watson GORDON	NG 847	Andrew GEDDES
NG 650	Sir John Watson GORDON	NG 848	Andrew GEDDES
NG 651	Angelica KAUFFMANN	NG 902	John James WILSON
NG 652	Hugh CAMERON	NG 903	Sir Henry RAEBURN
NG 657	George Paul CHALMERS	NG 909	Frederick de MOUCHERON
NG 660	Henry BONE	NG 910	ITALIAN School
NG 661	Henry BONE	NG 911	John OPIE
NG 663	Dirk SANTVOORT	NG 912	Jan BOTH
NG 664	Alexis GRIMOU	NG 913	Jan BOTH
NG 672	John Wilson EWBANK	NG 914	John HOUSTON
NG 675	Henry William PICKERSGILL	NG 915	James Eckford LAUDER
NG 681	Sir Henry RAEBURN	NG 916	Franz von LENBACH
NG 689	Jacopo TINTORETTO	NG 919	Sir George HARVEY
NG 690	VENETIAN School	NG 920	Joseph Thorburn ROSS
NG 691	Frans HALS	NG 924	George Paul CHALMERS
NG 692	Frans HALS	NG 925	Erskine NICOL
NG 704	VENETIAN School	NG 926	George WATSON
NG 707	Thomas DUNCAN	NG 927	George WATSON
NG 708	William SIMSON	NG 929	Revd John THOMSON
NG 720	George WATSON	NG 930	Sir Henry RAEBURN
NG 779	Sir William Fettes DOUGLAS	NG 931	John Sell COTMAN
NG 780	Alexander CARSE	NG 932	George Frederic WATTS
NG 786	John Christian SCHETKY	NG 933	Willem van de VELDE the Elder
NG 789	Imitator of George MORLAND	NG 934	Robert HERDMAN
NG 790	Alexander RUNCIMAN	NG 938	Robert BROUGH
NG 792	John RUNCIMAN	NG 942	James CHARLES
NG 793	John RUNCIMAN	NG 944	John CROME
NG 794	Conrad MEYER	NG 945	William Ewart LOCKHART
NG 795	Andrea SOLDI	NG 946	Allan RAMSAY
NG 796	David SCOTT	NG 948	Arthur MELVILLE
NG 799	Frederic Edwin CHURCH	NG 949	Sir George HARVEY
NG 801	Samuel BOUGH	NG 950	Sir David WILKIE
NG 805	Andrew SOMERVILLE	NG 951	Isack van OSTADE
NG 812	ITALIAN School	NG 952	VITALE da Bologna
NG 819	Samuel BOUGH	NG 953	Style of Benozzo GOZZOLI
NG 820	Allan RAMSAY	NG 957	Thomas GRAHAM
NG 823	David TENIERS the Younger	NG 958	George JAMESONE
NG 824	Jan Daemen COOL	NG 959	Jean-Siméon CHARDIN
NG 825	David SCOTT	NG 960	Circle of John Sell COTMAN
NG 826	After Simon VOUET	NG 961	Adolphe-Joseph MONTICELLI
NG 827	REMBRANDT	NG 962	Follower of CLAUDE LORRAIN
NG 828	Style of Francesco GUARDI	NG 966	Cecil Gordon LAWSON
NG 829	Style of Francesco GUARDI	NG 969	William Bell SCOTT
NG 831	Sir Henry RAEBURN	NG 970	William Gouw FERGUSON
NG 836	John PHILLIP	NG 980	James HOLLAND
NG 837	Sir Henry RAEBURN	NG 981	Sir William Fettes DOUGLAS
NG 838	William HOGARTH	NG 982	William KIDD

NG 987	John Milne DONALD	NG 1050	Jacob MARIS
NG 989	DUTCH School	NG 1051	Jacob MARIS
NG 990	Emanuel de WITTE	NG 1052	Jacob MARIS
NG 991	Pieter POURBUS	NG 1053	Willem MARIS
NG 992	David SCOTT	NG 1054	Emile van MARCKE
NG 993	George MORLAND	NG 1055	Emile van MARCKE
NG 994	George MORLAND	NG 1056	Anton MAUVE
NG 995	Bernard van ORLEY	NG 1057	Anton MAUVE
NG 998	GERMAN School	NG 1058	Anton MAUVE
NG 999	GERMAN School	NG 1059	Jozef ISRAËLS
NG 1000	Alexander Hohenlohe BURR	NG 1060	Jozef ISRAËLS
NG 1001	John BURR	NG 1061	Jozef ISRAËLS
NG 1002	Sir William Fettes DOUGLAS	NG 1062	Hendrik Johannes
NG 1003	Robert Scott LAUDER		WEISSENBRUCH
NG 1004	John PHILLIP	NG 1063	David FARQUHARSON
NG 1005	John RUNCIMAN	NG 1071	William McTAGGART
NG 1006	David SCOTT	NG 1072	Eugène BOUDIN
NG 1007	John Wilson EWBANK	NG 1076	Charles-François DAUBIGNY
NG 1013	Jan van GOYEN	NG 1130	Marcellin DESBOUTIN
NG 1014	Pieter van BLOEMEN	NG 1131	John PETTIE
NG 1017	Richard Parkes BONINGTON	NG 1133	Jules BASTIEN-LEPAGE
NG 1018	Sir William Quiller	NG 1135	John Sell COTMAN
	ORCHARDSON	NG 1138	Sir William Quiller
NG 1019	Albert MOORE		ORCHARDSON
NG 1020	Sir William Fettes DOUGLAS	NG 1139	Paolo VERONESE
NG 1021	Attributed to Gonzalo PÉREZ	NG 1142	John FAED
NG 1022	Adolphe-Joseph MONTICELLI	NG 1146	James Campbell NOBLE
NG 1023	MATTEO di Giovanni	NG 1147	David SCOTT
NG 1024	Paulus MOREELSE	NG 1155	John PHILLIP
NG 1026	After Sir Henry RAEBURN	NG 1187	John PETTIE
NG 1027	Sir Henry RAEBURN	NG 1188	Alexander FRASER the Younger
NG 1028	Georges MICHEL	NG 1189	Mariano FORTUNY
NG 1029	William Gouw FERGUSON	NG 1190	Giovanni Battista CIMA da
NG 1030	Cosimo ROSSELLI		Conegliano
NG 1032	Sir David WILKIE	NG 1192	Sir Henry RAEBURN
NG 1033	Constant TROYON	NG 1193 A	Sir George HARVEY
NG 1034	Constant TROYON	NG 1193 B	Sir George HARVEY
NG 1035	Charles-François DAUBIGNY	NG 1193 C	Sir George HARVEY
NG 1036	Charles-François DAUBIGNY	NG 1193 D	Sir George HARVEY
NG 1037	Camille COROT	NG 1193 E	Sir George HARVEY
NG 1038	Camille COROT	NG 1193 F	Sir George HARVEY
NG 1039	Follower of Camille COROT	NG 1199	Sir Henry RAEBURN
NG 1040	Jules DUPRÉ	NG 1200	Frans HALS
NG 1041	Jules DUPRÉ	NG 1201	William McTAGGART
NG 1042	Narcisse DIAZ de la Peña	NG 1202	Thomas COUTURE
NG 1043	Narcisse DIAZ de la Peña	NG 1206	James A. S. TORRANCE
NG 1044	Narcisse DIAZ de la Peña	NG 1207	Sir William Quiller
NG 1045	Alexandre-Gabriel DECAMPS		ORCHARDSON
NG 1046	Charles JACQUE	NG 1208	Robert NOBLE
NG 1047	Stanislas LÉPINE	NG 1210	Follower of Andrea del CASTAGNO
NG 1048	Henri HARPIGNIES	NG 1211	Gaspar de CRAYER
NG 1049	Jacob MARIS	NG 1215	Sir Joshua REYNOLDS

NG 1216	John HOPPNER	NG 1478	George Paul CHALMERS
NG 1218	John Crawford WINTOUR	NG 1479	Sir William Fettes DOUGLAS
NG 1219	John CONSTABLE	NG 1480	Alexander FRASER the Younger
NG 1222	Sir Henry RAEBURN	NG 1481	Alexander FRASER the Younger
NG 1223	Sir Henry RAEBURN	NG 1482	William McTAGGART
NG 1224	Sir Henry RAEBURN	NG 1483	William McTAGGART
NG 1225	Sir Henry RAEBURN	NG 1487	Sir James Lawton WINGATE
NG 1226	John EMMS	NG 1488	Sir James Lawton WINGATE
NG 1228	Revd John THOMSON	NG 1489	John Crawford WINTOUR
NG 1229	Sir William Quiller ORCHARDSON	NG 1490	John Crawford WINTOUR
		NG 1492	Paul BRIL
NG 1230	Sir Joseph Noel PATON	NG 1493	Abraham van CALRAET
NG 1231	James Elder CHRISTIE	NG 1496	François, Baron GÉRARD
NG 1236	Sir Henry RAEBURN	NG 1497	After Jan van GOYEN
NG 1250	Imitator of Francesco PESELLINO	NG 1498	Francesco GUARDI
NG 1252	Joos van CLEVE	NG 1499	Francesco GUARDI
NG 1253	Follower of GEERTGEN tot Sint Jans	NG 1500	Jan de BRAIJ
		NG 1501	Jan de BRAIJ
NG 1254	NETHERLANDISH School	NG 1502	Jan de BRAIJ
NG 1372	Cecil Gordon LAWSON	NG 1503	Jan de BRAIJ
NG 1383	Alexander NASMYTH	NG 1504	Simon LUTTICHUYS
NG 1444	Hugh CAMERON	NG 1505	Jan Davidsz. de HEEM
NG 1445	Sir David WILKIE	NG 1506	Meindert HOBBEMA
NG 1446	After Matthias STOM	NG 1507	Sir Peter LELY
NG 1447	Camille COROT	NG 1508	Herman SAFTLEVEN
NG 1448	Camille COROT	NG 1509	Nicolaes MAES
NG 1449	Camille COROT	NG 1510	DUTCH School
NG 1450	Camille COROT	NG 1511	Studio of Jacopo BASSANO
NG 1451	Attributed to Camille COROT	NG 1512	Follower of Gaspard DUGHET
NG 1452	Attributed to Camille COROT	NG 1513	Giovanni SERODINE
NG 1453	Charles-François DAUBIGNY	NG 1515	Follower of Egbert van HEEMSKERCK
NG 1454	Narcisse DIAZ de la Peña		
NG 1455	Henri FANTIN-LATOUR	NG 1516	Gaspar Pieter VERBRUGGEN the Younger
NG 1456	Henri FANTIN-LATOUR		
NG 1457	Charles JACQUE	NG 1517	Gaspar Pieter VERBRUGGEN the Younger
NG 1458	Stanislas LÉPINE		
NG 1459	Attributed to Stanislas LÉPINE	NG 1521	Thomas GAINSBOROUGH
NG 1461	Georges MICHEL	NG 1522	Sir Thomas LAWRENCE
NG 1462	Adolphe-Joseph MONTICELLI	NG 1523	Allan RAMSAY
NG 1463	Adolphe-Joseph MONTICELLI	NG 1524	Allan RAMSAY
NG 1464	Adolphe-Joseph MONTICELLI	NG 1527	Sir David WILKIE
NG 1465	Adolphe-Joseph MONTICELLI	NG 1528	Attributed to Giuliano AMIDEI
NG 1466	Constant TROYON	NG 1535	FERRARESE School
NG 1467	Antoine VOLLON	NG 1536	Studio of Sandro BOTTICELLI
NG 1468	Johannes BOSBOOM	NG 1537	Jan PROVOST
NG 1469	Johannes BOSBOOM	NG 1538	Attributed to Jacopo del SELLAIO
NG 1471	Jacob MARIS	NG 1539 A	MASTER of the SAN LUCCHESE ALTARPIECE
NG 1473	Albert NEUHUIJS		
NG 1474	Albert NEUHUIJS	NG 1539 B	MASTER of the SAN LUCCHESE ALTARPIECE
NG 1475	Samuel BOUGH		
NG 1476	Samuel BOUGH	NG 1540 A	MASTER of 1419
NG 1477	George Paul CHALMERS	NG 1540 B	MASTER of 1419

NG 1541 NETHERLANDISH School
NG 1544 NETHERLANDISH School
NG 1564 Jan LIEVENS
NG 1565 Workshop of SANO di Pietro
NG 1579 Attributed to Sir George HARVEY
NG 1614 Joseph Mallord William TURNER
NG 1616 Honoré DAUMIER
NG 1618 Imitator of Edouard MANET
NG 1623 Alphonse LEGROS
NG 1625 After Diego VELÁZQUEZ
NG 1628 Francisco de GOYA y Lucientes
NG 1629 George Paul CHALMERS
NG 1633 Style of PIERO di Cosimo
NG 1634 EMILIAN School
NG 1635 Studio of Jacopo BASSANO
NG 1636 After Jacopo BASSANO
NG 1637 Follower of Joseph VERNET
NG 1638 ITALIAN School
NG 1642 NETHERLANDISH School
NG 1643 Paul GAUGUIN
NG 1647 David SCOTT
NG 1648 Robert ALEXANDER
NG 1649 Sir James Lawton WINGATE
NG 1651 Claude MONET
NG 1655 Edward Arthur WALTON
NG 1656 John Singer SARGENT
NG 1657 After William HOGARTH
NG 1658 Sir William Quiller ORCHARDSON
NG 1659 William McTAGGART
NG 1663 John PHILLIP
NG 1666 Sir Joshua REYNOLDS
NG 1667 FRENCH School
NG 1669 William Darling McKAY
NG 1670 Johannes VERMEER
NG 1673 Francesco MARMITTA
NG 1674 George ROMNEY
NG 1675 Attributed to Vincenzo CATENA
NG 1676 David SCOTT
NG 1677 Sir William ALLAN
NG 1678 Follower of Joos van CLEVE
NG 1679 Sir Daniel MACNEE
NG 1681 Camille COROT
NG 1686 DUTCH School
NG 1692 William STOTT
NG 1714 Imitator of Richard WILSON
NG 1717 Hugh CAMERON
NG 1718 David MARTIN
NG 1719 Attributed to Marco ZOPPO
NG 1720 Sir David WILKIE
NG 1721 Dante Gabriel Charles ROSSETTI
NG 1725 After Sir David WILKIE
NG 1727 Revd John THOMSON
NG 1728 FLEMISH School
NG 1729 James ARCHER
NG 1730 Hugh CAMERON
NG 1731 Sir William Fettes DOUGLAS
NG 1732 Charles Hodge MACKIE
NG 1733 Alexander Ignatius ROCHE
NG 1734 Sir James Lawton WINGATE
NG 1738 Studio of Giovanni TOSCANI
NG 1739 Pierre PUVIS DE CHAVANNES
NG 1740 Sir George REID
NG 1743 Attributed to Samuel OWEN
NG 1744 James Abbot McNeill WHISTLER
NG 1745 ITALIAN School
NG 1746 Studio of Bernardino BUTINONE
NG 1749 William Borthwick JOHNSTONE
NG 1751 David SCOTT
NG 1752 William MOSMAN
NG 1757 William McTAGGART
NG 1758 Filippino LIPPI
NG 1759 John BURNET
NG 1762 Sir Henry RAEBURN
NG 1763 Hugh CAMERON
NG 1764 Hugh CAMERON
NG 1765 David MUIRHEAD
NG 1768 James NORIE
NG 1769 James NORIE
NG 1776 Peter de WINT
NG 1784 John ALEXANDER
NG 1785 Edgar DEGAS
NG 1786 Anthony Vandyke Copley FIELDING
NG 1787 John Singer SARGENT
NG 1788 George Frederic WATTS
NG 1792 After Sandro BOTTICELLI
NG 1798 John ALEXANDER
NG 1799 William Darling McKAY
NG 1800 William Darling McKAY
NG 1801 David MUIRHEAD
NG 1802 William MILLAR
NG 1803 Vincent van GOGH
NG 1804 Robert McINNES
NG 1805 Pietro PERUGINO
NG 1814 Edward Atkinson HORNEL
NG 1815 Edward Atkinson HORNEL
NG 1816 Sir Henry RAEBURN
NG 1817 A Sir Daniel MACNEE
NG 1817 B Sir Daniel MACNEE
NG 1817 C Sir Daniel MACNEE
NG 1818 A Sir Daniel MACNEE
NG 1818 B Sir Daniel MACNEE
NG 1819 A Sir Daniel MACNEE

NG 1819 B	Sir Daniel MACNEE	NG 1894	Patrick NASMYTH
NG 1819 C	Sir Daniel MACNEE	NG 1895	Bernard van ORLEY
NG 1820	Sir Daniel MACNEE	NG 1896	Sir William Fettes DOUGLAS
NG 1821	Sir Daniel MACNEE	NG 1897	Jacob MORE
NG 1822	Sir Daniel MACNEE	NG 1904	Bernardo DADDI
NG 1824	BRITISH School	NG 1906	William McTAGGART
NG 1825	Walter GEIKIE	NG 1907	William McTAGGART
NG 1828	Alexander CARSE	NG 1912	Elizabeth NASMYTH
NG 1829	FRENCH School	NG 1915	William York MacGREGOR
NG 1832	DUTCH School	NG 1921	Sir Daniel MACNEE
NG 1833	Formerly attributed to James HAMILTON	NG 1923	Sir Henry RAEBURN
NG 1834	William McTAGGART	NG 1924	Andrew WILSON
NG 1835	George MORLAND	NG 1926	Attributed to David MARTIN
NG 1836	George MORLAND	NG 1927	After Hans ASPER
NG 1837	John Thomas SETON	NG 1928 A	GERMAN School
NG 1839	Henry G. DUGUID	NG 1928 B	GERMAN School
NG 1840	John Thomas SETON	NG 1929	NETHERLANDISH School
NG 1841	John Thomas SETON	NG 1930	Jean CLOUET
NG 1842	After Sir David WILKIE	NG 1931	POLIDORO da Lanciano
NG 1852	Camille COROT	NG 1932	DUTCH School
NG 1854	After RAPHAEL	NG 1933	Gerlach FLICKE
NG 1864	Revd John THOMSON	NG 1934	Gerlach FLICKE
NG 1865 A	Phoebe Anna TRAQUAIR	NG 1935	Formerly attributed to Allan RAMSAY
NG 1865 B	Phoebe Anna TRAQUAIR	NG 1937	Attributed to Pieter ROESTRAETEN
NG 1865 C	Phoebe Anna TRAQUAIR	NG 1938	Attributed to Willem KEY
NG 1865 D	Phoebe Anna TRAQUAIR	NG 1939	Attributed to Willem KEY
NG 1866	Phoebe Anna TRAQUAIR	NG 1940	Attributed to APOLLONIO di Giovanni
NG 1867 A	Phoebe Anna TRAQUAIR	NG 1941	Jacopo del SELLAIO
NG 1867 B	Phoebe Anna TRAQUAIR	NG 1942	Lucas CRANACH the Elder
NG 1867 C	Phoebe Anna TRAQUAIR	NG 1943	After BRONZINO
NG 1868	Phoebe Anna TRAQUAIR	NG 1944	After Sir Anthony van DYCK
NG 1869	Phoebe Anna TRAQUAIR	NG 1945	Jan WIJNANTS
NG 1871	Phoebe Anna TRAQUAIR	NG 1946	Ludolf BACKHUYZEN
NG 1873	El GRECO	NG 1947	Imitator of Willem van de VELDE the Younger
NG 1874	Arthur PERIGAL	NG 1948	Patrick NASMYTH
NG 1876	David SCOTT	NG 1950	Henri FANTIN-LATOUR
NG 1877	David SCOTT	NG 1951	John Macallan SWAN
NG 1878	Sir Henry RAEBURN	NG 1957	William York MacGREGOR
NG 1879	John Henry LORIMER	NG 1958	TUSCAN School
NG 1882	Cosmo ALEXANDER	NG 1960	Allan RAMSAY
NG 1883	Jean-Siméon CHARDIN	NG 1961	Style of Philippe MERCIER
NG 1884	Allan RAMSAY	NG 1962	Style of Philippe MERCIER
NG 1885	George WATSON	NG 1964	David Octavius HILL
NG 1886	Sir David MURRAY	NG 1966	William DENUNE
NG 1887	Alexander FRASER the Elder	NG 1967	Attributed to Andrew GEDDES
NG 1888	Alexander FRASER the Elder	NG 1968	Patrick NASMYTH
NG 1889	Allan RAMSAY	NG 1969	Imitator of Stanislas LÉPINE
NG 1890	Sir David WILKIE	NG 1973	UNKNOWN
NG 1891	George Paul CHALMERS		
NG 1892	Thomas Hope McLACHLAN		
NG 1893	Charlotte NASMYTH		

NG 1974	Workshop of APOLLONIO di Giovanni	NG 2103	Sir David WILKIE
NG 1975	MASTER of the ADIMARI CASSONE	NG 2104	Alexander NASMYTH
		NG 2106	James CADENHEAD
NG 1980	Alexander FRASER the Younger	NG 2107	Henri FANTIN-LATOUR
NG 1981	Patrick NASMYTH	NG 2108	Sir Henry RAEBURN
NG 1982	William WALLS	NG 2111	Sir James Lawton WINGATE
NG 1986	Peter GRAHAM	NG 2112	Sir Henry RAEBURN
NG 2014	Follower of CANALETTO	NG 2113	Sir George CHALMERS
NG 2015	George MORLAND	NG 2114	Sir David WILKIE
NG 2016	John CONSTABLE	NG 2115	John MARTIN
NG 2017	Sir James GUTHRIE	NG 2116	John RUNCIMAN
NG 2018	Sir James GUTHRIE	NG 2118	David SCOTT
NG 2022	Cosmo ALEXANDER	NG 2119	Allan RAMSAY
NG 2023	James PATERSON	NG 2120	Francesco MONTI
NG 2024	Ambrosius BENSON	NG 2121	Samuel BOUGH
NG 2028	John PHILLIP	NG 2123	Sir James Lawton WINGATE
NG 2032	Circle of Daniel MIJTENS the Elder	NG 2124	John SYME
NG 2033	John DUNCAN	NG 2125	John SYME
NG 2034	Sir Henry RAEBURN	NG 2126	David ALLAN
NG 2036	Anne FORBES	NG 2127	Andrew GEDDES
NG 2037	William DENUNE	NG 2129	CERANO
NG 2038	Charles Hodge MACKIE	NG 2130	Sir David WILKIE
NG 2039	Revd John THOMSON	NG 2131	Thomas HUDSON
NG 2040	Attributed to Jacob or Abel GRIMMER	NG 2133	Allan RAMSAY
		NG 2134	Alexander FRASER the Elder
NG 2041	George Frederic WATTS	NG 2135	Sir John LAVERY
NG 2043	John DUNCAN	NG 2136	Robert HERDMAN
NG 2044	Charles Hodge MACKIE	NG 2137	William McTAGGART
NG 2045	Sir George HARVEY	NG 2138	William McTAGGART
NG 2046	Sir George CLAUSEN	NG 2139	William McTAGGART
NG 2067	Sir John Everett MILLAIS	NG 2140	William McTAGGART
NG 2072	David SCOTT	NG 2141	John Crawford WINTOUR
NG 2073	David SCOTT	NG 2142	Sir James GUTHRIE
NG 2074	NETHERLANDISH School	NG 2143	Alexander Ignatius ROCHE
NG 2079	Sir David Young CAMERON	NG 2144	Arthur MELVILLE
NG 2080	Sir David Young CAMERON	NG 2145	Edward Atkinson HORNEL
NG 2081	Sir David Young CAMERON	NG 2146	James A. S. TORRANCE
NG 2086	William York MacGREGOR	NG 2147	Sir Henry RAEBURN
NG 2087	Sir James GUTHRIE	NG 2148	Sir Henry RAEBURN
NG 2088	Sir James GUTHRIE	NG 2149	Sir Henry RAEBURN
NG 2089	Sir George HARVEY	NG 2150	Sir Henry RAEBURN
NG 2090	Sir George HARVEY	NG 2151	Allan RAMSAY
NG 2091	Sir George HARVEY	NG 2152	Allan RAMSAY
NG 2092	Sir George HARVEY	NG 2156	Andrew GEDDES
NG 2096	William Gouw FERGUSON	NG 2157	David ALLAN
NG 2097	Sir Peter Paul RUBENS	NG 2158	William McTAGGART
NG 2098	Camille PISSARRO	NG 2159	Hans HYSING
NG 2099	Circle of Sandro BOTTICELLI	NG 2160	El GRECO
NG 2100	Alexander NASMYTH	NG 2161	Jacopo TINTORETTO and Studio
NG 2101	Patrick NASMYTH	NG 2162	Hugh CAMERON
NG 2102	Patrick NASMYTH	NG 2163	After John CONSTABLE
		NG 2164	Richard Parkes BONINGTON

NG 2165	Richard Parkes BONINGTON	NG 2240	CLAUDE Lorrain
NG 2166	William MÜLLER	NG 2249	Revd John THOMSON
NG 2170	Sir John Watson GORDON	NG 2253	Thomas GAINSBOROUGH
NG 2171	Sir Joshua REYNOLDS	NG 2254	Sir Daniel MACNEE
NG 2172	Sir David WILKIE	NG 2255	William Craig SHIRREFF
NG 2173	Sir David WILKIE	NG 2256	David ALLAN
NG 2174	Thomas GAINSBOROUGH	NG 2257	William YELLOWLEES
NG 2175	Alexander Garden SINCLAIR	NG 2258	William YELLOWLEES
NG 2176	Sir James GUTHRIE	NG 2259	Jan Daemen COOL
NG 2177	Sir John Watson GORDON	NG 2260	David ALLAN
NG 2179	Attributed to François BOUCHER	NG 2261	David ROBERTS
NG 2180	Diego VELÁZQUEZ	NG 2263	Revd John THOMSON
NG 2181	Sir Henry RAEBURN	NG 2264	Revd John THOMSON
NG 2182	Sir Henry RAEBURN	NG 2265	Revd John THOMSON
NG 2183	Sir Joshua REYNOLDS	NG 2266	Jean-Louis FORAIN
NG 2184	Sir William Quiller ORCHARDSON	NG 2267	William DYCE
		NG 2268	POPPI
NG 2185	William McTAGGART	NG 2269	Berthe MORISOT
NG 2186	William McTAGGART	NG 2270	After LEONARDO da Vinci
NG 2189	Alexander RUNCIMAN	NG 2271	LORENZO Monaco and Workshop
NG 2190	Eugène DELACROIX	NG 2272	Attributed to Francis WHEATLEY
NG 2191	Revd John THOMSON	NG 2273	Quentin MASSYS
NG 2193	Sir Peter Paul RUBENS	NG 2274	FRENCH School
NG 2194	Robert GIBB	NG 2275	Frans POURBUS the Elder
NG 2195	Robert GIBB	NG 2276	Giulio Cesare PROCACCINI
NG 2196	Sir David WILKIE	NG 2281	Adam ELSHEIMER
NG 2197	Sir David WILKIE	NG 2283	Claude MONET
NG 2198	Sir David WILKIE	NG 2284	Sir James GUTHRIE
NG 2199	William DYCE	NG 2291	BACCHIACCA
NG 2200	William York MacGREGOR	NG 2292	David ALLAN
NG 2201	Sir Daniel MACNEE	NG 2293	Andrew GEDDES
NG 2206	Paul CÉZANNE	NG 2295	Allan RAMSAY
NG 2212	John SMIBERT	NG 2296	Sir Henry RAEBURN
NG 2213	Gerard DAVID	NG 2297	Andrea del SARTO
NG 2214	William McTAGGART	NG 2298	John POWELL
NG 2215	Sir William Quiller ORCHARDSON	NG 2299	SCOTTISH School
		NG 2301	Sir Henry RAEBURN
NG 2216	Vincent van GOGH	NG 2302	Sir David WILKIE
NG 2217	Vincent van GOGH	NG 2303	George CHINNERY
NG 2220	Paul GAUGUIN	NG 2306	James WARD
NG 2221	Paul GAUGUIN	NG 2307	James WARD
NG 2222	Georges SEURAT	NG 2308	Sir George HARVEY
NG 2224	Edgar DEGAS	NG 2309	John CROME
NG 2225	Edgar DEGAS	NG 2310	GERMAN School
NG 2227	Edgar DEGAS	NG 2311	Sir Peter Paul RUBENS
NG 2230	Auguste RENOIR	NG 2312	Adam ELSHEIMER
NG 2232	Gustave COURBET	NG 2313	DOMENICHINO
NG 2233	Gustave COURBET	NG 2314	Aelbert CUYP
NG 2234	Gustave COURBET	NG 2315	Sir David WILKIE
NG 2235	Alfred SISLEY	NG 2316	Robert Scott LAUDER
NG 2236	Paul CÉZANNE	NG 2317	Attributed to François QUESNEL
NG 2238	Giovanni Battista PITTONI	NG 2318	Gaspard DUGHET

NG 2319	Nicolas POUSSIN	NG 2349	Eugène BOUDIN
NG 2320	Andrew GEDDES	NG 2350	Eugène BOUDIN
NG 2324	Georges SEURAT	NG 2351	Eugène BOUDIN
NG 2325	Pietro TESTA	NG 2352	Alexander FRASER the Younger
NG 2326	After Pietro TESTA	NG 2353	Sir James GUTHRIE
NG 2333	Robert Gemmell HUTCHISON	NG 2354	Sir James GUTHRIE
NG 2334	William Stewart MacGEORGE	NG 2355	William McTAGGART
NG 2335	Walter GEIKIE	NG 2356	William McTAGGART
NG 2337	Sir David WILKIE	NG 2357	James PATERSON
NG 2338	Attributed to Andrea del VERROCCHIO and Workshop	NG 2358	Sir James Lawton WINGATE
		NG 2359	Sir James Lawton WINGATE
NG 2339	Gavin HAMILTON	NG 2360	Alexander Ignatius ROCHE
NG 2340	Sir George CLAUSEN	NG 2361	George HENRY
NG 2347	Giovanni Battista MORONI	NG 2366	Richard WAITT
NG 2348	Edward Arthur WALTON		

Acquisitions since publication of the last catalogue

NG 2367	William Bell SCOTT	NG 2405	Eugène DELACROIX
NG 2368	William Bell SCOTT	NG 2406	Eugène BOUDIN
NG 2369	Pompeo Girolamo BATONI	NG 2407	Hans HOLBEIN the Younger
NG 2370	Francesco GUARDI	NG 2408	Edward Arthur WALTON
NG 2371	Eugène BOUDIN	NG 2409	William DYCE
NG 2372	Eugène BOUDIN	NG 2410	William DYCE
NG 2373	Eugène BOUDIN	NG 2411	William McTAGGART
NG 2374	Attributed to Eugène BOUDIN	NG 2412	Revd John THOMSON
NG 2375	Guido RENI	NG 2413	Pieter Jansz. SAENREDAM
NG 2376	Peter GRAHAM	NG 2414	John PETTIE
NG 2377	Meindert HOBBEMA	NG 2415	William McTAGGART
NG 2378	Attributed to PIETRO da Cortona	NG 2417	John PETTIE
NG 2379	Robert Gemmell HUTCHISON	NG 2418	Lorenzo LOTTO
NG 2380	Sir William ALLAN	NG 2419	Jacopo TINTORETTO
NG 2381	James ARCHER	NG 2420	Gerrit DOU
NG 2382	David MUIRHEAD	NG 2421	Jan STEEN
NG 2383	Sir David Young CAMERON	NG 2422	Sir William Quiller ORCHARDSON
NG 2384	Camille PISSARRO		
NG 2385	Claude MONET	NG 2423	Claude MONET
NG 2386	Alfred SISLEY	NG 2424	James PATERSON
NG 2390	Adolphe-Joseph MONTICELLI	NG 2425	James FAED
NG 2391	Adolphe-Joseph MONTICELLI	NG 2426	Attributed to François CLOUET
NG 2392	Eugène BOUDIN	NG 2427	MASTER of the FEMALE HALF-LENGTHS
NG 2393	Bessie MacNICOL		
NG 2394	Sir Henry RAEBURN	NG 2428	Gavin HAMILTON
NG 2395	William DYCE	NG 2429	Robert Scott LAUDER
NG 2396	William Bell SCOTT	NG 2430	Sir David WILKIE
NG 2397	Sir Peter Paul RUBENS	NG 2431	Sir John LAVERY
NG 2398	GIULIO Romano	NG 2432	Henri HARPIGNIES
NG 2399	Claude MONET	NG 2433	Sir David WILKIE
NG 2400	Sir William ALLAN	NG 2434	Philips KONINCK
NG 2404	Thomas WARRENDER	NG 2435	James Eckford LAUDER

NG 2437	Robert McGREGOR	NG 2543	Alexander RUNCIMAN
NG 2438	Andrew GEDDES	NG 2544	Alexander RUNCIMAN
NG 2440	François BOUCHER	NG 2545	Allan RAMSAY
NG 2441	François BOUCHER	NG 2546	Alexander NASMYTH
NG 2442	François BOUCHER	NG 2547	William KIDD
NG 2443	Sir David Young CAMERON	NG 2548	François-Xavier FABRE
NG 2444	Maximilien LUCE	NG 2549	Thomas FAED
NG 2446	Joseph BIDAULD	NG 2557	John KNOX
NG 2447	Denys CALVAERT	NG 2558	Noël HALLÉ
NG 2448	Benjamin WEST	NG 2560	Thomas FAED
NG 2450	Robert BURNS	NG 2562	Adolf SENFF
NG 2451	Emilius Ditlev BAERENTZEN	NG 2563	Nicolaas VERKOLJE
NG 2452	Sir Stanley CURSITER	NG 2581	John PHILLIP
NG 2453	Honoré DAUMIER	NG 2583	George HENRY
NG 2454	George HENRY	NG 2584	Attributed to CORREGGIO
NG 2455	Sir David Young CAMERON	NG 2585	William DYCE
NG 2456	Horatio McCULLOCH	NG 2586	Charles-François DAUBIGNY
NG 2457	Alexander Ignatius ROCHE	NG 2587	Horatio McCULLOCH
NG 2458	Pollock Sinclair NISBET	NG 2588	Antoine VESTIER
NG 2459	John CROME	NG 2589	Pompeo Girolamo BATONI
NG 2461	François, Baron GÉRARD	NG 2591	Achille-Etna MICHALLON
NG 2462	Paul-Camille GUIGOU	NG 2593	Anicet-Charles-Gabriel
NG 2463	William Darling McKAY		LEMONNIER
NG 2464	Gawen HAMILTON	NG 2614	SCOTTISH School
NG 2465	Jean-Victor BERTIN	NG 2623	Sebastiano RICCI
NG 2466	Sir Stanley CURSITER	NG 2627	Alexander NASMYTH
NG 2490	Robert BURNS	NG 2634	John FAED
NG 2491	El GRECO	NG 2635	Pierre SUBLEYRAS
NG 2493	Sir George CHALMERS	NG 2636	Robert HERDMAN
NG 2494	CARIANI	NG 2637	William McTAGGART
NG 2495	Godfried SCHALCKEN	NG 2638	William McTAGGART
NG 2505	Christen KØBKE	NG 2639	William McTAGGART
NG 2511	William McTAGGART	NG 2640	William McTAGGART
NG 2516	Goffredo WALS	NG 2641	Sir George HARVEY
NG 2518	Jacob MORE	NG 2642	Joseph BIDAULD
NG 2520	Andrew WILSON	NG 2647	Giulio Cesare PROCACCINI
NG 2523	Jan WEENIX	NG 2650	H. PEATTIE
NG 2524	François BONVIN	NG 2651	Paris BORDON
NG 2526	Louis GAUFFIER	NG 2652	André GIROUX
NG 2527	John FAED	NG 2653	Imitator of Adam ELSHEIMER
NG 2528	William McTAGGART	NG 2655	Phoebe Anna TRAQUAIR
NG 2541	John James NAPIER	NG 2656	GUERCINO
NG 2542	Alexander NASMYTH		

LIST OF ALTERED ATTRIBUTIONS

Altered since the 1978 Shorter Catalogue

NG 3   *from* Bassano *to* VENETIAN School
NG 21   *from* Neapolitan *to* ROMAN School
NG 56   *from* Italian *to* Bernardo CASTELLO
NG 78   *from* Hemessen *to* NETHERLANDISH School
NG 83   *from* Novelli *to* Studio of Jusepe de RIBERA
NG 84   *from* Neapolitan *to* Follower of Jusepe de RIBERA
NG 88   *from* Dughet *to* Attributed to Carlo Antonio TAVELLA
NG 101   *from* Flemish *to* NETHERLANDISH School
NG 108   *from* Italian *to* FLEMISH School
NG 305   *from* J. Runciman *to* Sir John Baptiste de MEDINA
NG 376   *from* Van de Velde *to* Hendrik van MINDERHOUT
NG 432   *from* Murillo *to* SPANISH School
NG 458   *from* Poussin *to* After Giovanni BELLINI
NG 619   *from* Dutch *to* Christian Wilhelm DIETRICH
NG 645   *from* Italian *to* FLORENTINE School
NG 794   *from* Dutch *to* Conrad MEYER
NG 824   *from* Cuyp *to* Jan Daemen COOL
NG 826   *from* French *to* Copy after Simon VOUET
NG 844   *from* Crome *to* Attributed to David HODGSON
NG 902   *from* John Wilson *to* John James WILSON
NG 982   *from* Fraser *to* William KIDD
NG 1014   *from* Asselijn *to* Pieter van BLOEMEN
NG 1254   *from* Flemish *to* NETHERLANDISH School
NG 1515   *from* Tilborch *to* Follower of Egbert van HEEMSKERCK
NG 1541   *from* Flemish *to* NETHERLANDISH School
NG 1544   *from* Flemish *to* NETHERLANDISH School
NG 1638   *from* Imitator of Alessandro Longhi *to* ITALIAN School
NG 1642   *from* Flemish *to* NETHERLANDISH School
NG 1667   *from* Delacroix *to* FRENCH School
NG 1745   *from* Ferrarese *to* ITALIAN School
NG 1829   *from* G. Hamilton *to* FRENCH School
NG 1929   *from* Flemish *to* NETHERLANDISH School
NG 1973   *from* Jamesone *to* UNKNOWN
NG 2032   *from* Scougall *to* Circle of Daniel MIJTENS
NG 2074   *from* Flemish *to* NETHERLANDISH School
NG 2099   *from* Lippi *to* Circle of Sandro BOTTICELLI
NG 2179   *from* French *to* Attributed to François BOUCHER
NG 2259   *from* Cuyp *to* Jan Daemen COOL

Altered from the 1993 Paxton House Catalogue

NG 21   *from* Neapolitan School *to* ROMAN SCHOOL
NG 432   *from* Bolognese School *to* SPANISH School

Altered from the 1993 Italian and Spanish Paintings Catalogue

NG 3   *from* Attributed to Bassano *to* VENETIAN School
NG 21   *from* Neapolitan School *to* ROMAN School
NG 83   *from* Novelli *to* Studio of Jusepe de RIBERA
NG 84   *from* Neapolitan School *to* Follower of Jusepe de RIBERA
NG 645   *from* Italian School *to* FLORENTINE School
NG 1745 *from* Ferrarese School *to* ITALIAN School